Other books by Karl Haffner

The Cure for Soul Fatigue

Pilgrim's Problems

The Cure for the Last Daze

Out of the Hot Tub, Into the World

Karl Haffner, Ph.D.

Pacific Press® Publishing Association
Nampa, Idaho
Oshawa, Ontario, Canada
www.pacificpress.com

Designed by Mark Bond
Cover art by iStockphoto

Additional copies of this book are available by calling toll free
1-800-765-6955 or by ordering online at
www.adventistbookcenter.com

ISBN: 0-8163-2150-7
ISBN 13:9780816321506

06 07 08 09 10 · 5 4 3 2 1

Dedicated to the Jones and Dawes Families

In loving memory of Jenda Jones . . .
a dynamo who could light up a gym
with her smile and her play.
She was always a recharge
to my soul.

"May the God of hope fill
you with all joy and peace
as you trust in him,
so that you may overflow
with hope by the power of the
Holy Spirit"
(Romans 15:13. NIV).

Table of Contents

INTRODUCTION

SOUL QUESTIONS

SOUL PAIN

SOUL COMMUNITY

SOUL GOODNESS

CONCLUSION

Introduction

Ask almost anyone, "How are you?" If they elaborate beyond "Fine," chances are you'll hear a litany like this: "I'm *sooooo* busy. I take the kids to soccer on Tuesdays and Thursdays; then the kids have music lessons. I'm volunteering at the church. I slept only two hours last night because I am so behind on a project at work . . ."

When is the last time you heard someone answer the question "How are you?" by saying, "I'm OK—except that I just have too much free time"? Imagine someone explaining, "I've reflected on my most deeply held values, so I carve out significant chunks of time each day in order to live out my priorities. God is important to me, so I spend a lot time nurturing my relationship with Him. And I value my family, so I commit time each day to my spouse and my kids. Beyond that, I just don't know what to do with myself. My soul is so rested I feel like a bear in hibernation. I'm at perfect peace."

Who really lives like that?

Here's the better question: Why not?

It is possible to live your most deeply held values. You don't need to wait for the kids to leave home or a better boss to fix the workplace or your cholesterol to drop to one hundred. Today, you can choose to synchronize your values with your real life.

To do this, however, you must choose to cheat—as author and pastor Andy Stanley points out. By cheating, however, he's not talking about behaving unethically. It's not a call to be like the Nebraska football player who was confronted by his professor for cheating. The teacher explained, "You flunked the final even though you only missed one problem."

"Then how could I have flunked?" the student asked.

"Well," the professor said, "you've been flunking all semester, and you are sitting next to the top student in the class. He also got one problem wrong."

"But that could just be a coincidence," the football player insisted.

"But you both missed the same problem."

"Well, that could be a coincidence, too."

"Yes, but the straight A student wrote next to the question, 'I don't know the answer to this question,' and you wrote, 'I don't know the answer to this question either.' "

That's not the kind of cheating we're talking about here. Rather, the idea is that we all have to forfeit certain opportunities in order to take advantage of other ones. In other words, no one can excel in every arena of life.

We try. Oh, do we try! We cram our calendars with every opportunity that presents itself. The result? Souls that feel like rag dolls caught in the washer's spin cycle.

It's no wonder that soul fatigue has reached epidemic proportions in our day. Weariness of spirit is the norm anymore. This explains why my publisher approached me with a request to write this sequel to my book *The Cure for Soul Fatigue.* (I guess the first offering wasn't quite the panacea promised!) It helps me to understand why the members of my congregation consistently choose "soul fatigue" as the topic they most want to hear addressed from the pulpit. This clarifies why people tend to moan on and on about their busyness when asked the simple question, "How are you?" Let's face it: We live in a world of weary folk. People are stressed out, worn out, and burned out.

So what's a person to do? The only answer is to cheat. The truth is, of course, you're already cheating in some arenas. Your boss, your spouse, your kids, your God, your health, your yard, your bank account, your handicap at the country club—corners will get cut. The key to addressing matters of the soul is to be intentional about cheating. And only you can decide for you.

Andy Stanley explains: "Everybody cheats. This principle is already at work in your life . . . one way or another. When you put it to work *for* you, it has the power to transform every facet of your life. When we choose to cheat in accordance with God's priorities for our lives, it is an invitation for Him to bless us in ways we never dared to imagine."[1]

So where will you cheat? Equally important is gaining clarity on where you're *not* going to cheat. You've got to know what is most important.

Tennessee Titans center Kevin Long, who played under Coach Bobby Bowden at Florida State University, said his college coach inspired the team with parables. Long's favorite story reminds us that knowing what's most important is the key to success:

Bowden was playing college baseball, but he had never hit a home run. Finally he drilled one down the right-field line, into the corner. He barreled around first and eyed the third base coach who was frantically waving like a windmill in a hurricane. He circled second, and then rounded third, and raced toward home. Triumphantly he waved to the cheering fans as he trotted to the dugout. Then the pitcher tossed the ball to the first baseman, and the umpire screamed, "He's out at first!"

Coach Bowden said, "If you don't take care of first base, it doesn't matter what you do. If you don't honor the Lord first, it doesn't matter what else you do."[2]

Cheat the Lord, and you will strike out in life. Unfortunately too many people learn this the hard way. John Grisham, the award-winning novelist, tells of learning this after graduating from Mississippi State University. One of his classmates in law school told John he was terminally ill. The author asked him: "What do you do when you realize you are about to die?"

The friend replied, "It's real simple. You get things right with God, and you spend as much time with those you love as you can. Then you settle up with everybody else."[3]

Not a bad recipe for life, huh? Perhaps we can cook it up together as we embark on this journey through the landscape of the soul. Let's do it before the doctor comes with a terminal diagnosis.

At the outset you need to know that it is possible to live a sane and balanced life. You can embody your deepest values. You can cheat the trivial time-suckers that rob you of life. You can imbibe the fullness of God's kingdom—here and now.

Hang with me, and we'll explore God's Word in a quest to clarify values. Along the way we'll address some of the big issues that relate to the soul: questions, pain, community, and goodness. Read on, because soul matters.

1. Andy Stanley, *Choosing to Cheat* (Nashville: Thomas Nelson Publishers, 2002), p. xii.

2. *The Tennessean* (9-29-00), adapted from <http://preachingtoday.com/illustrations/article_print.html?id=23744>.

3. *Direction* (August, 2003), quoted on <http://www.preachingtoday.com>.

Soul Questions

"The soul is like a ship in a narrow

river which does not have room to

turn. It is always running aground

and foundering in the shallows. But

Jesus Christ is in every way sufficient

to the vast desires of the soul. In Him

the soul may spread all its sails with

no fear of touching bottom."

(John Flavel, 1630–1691)

—Chapter one—
Answering Life's Biggest Questions

When were you born? Easy answer, right? Because a birthday is a big deal.

Some years ago I was at a conference in Brisbane, Australia, just getting ready to stand up to speak, when my wife handed me the video camera and said, "Check this out." I peered into the viewfinder and watched a clip of her holding a sign that said, "ARE YOU FREE JUNE 4, 2000? I'LL NEED YOUR HELP IN THE DELIVERY ROOM!"

My heart stopped. Just then I heard someone introducing me to start my sermon! I've never preached more irrational gobbledygook in my life because my brain was on a birthday.

Another question: *Where* were you born? I don't have to think to answer that one, either. I was born in Plentywood, Montana, population 2,328. That's right, my roots are in a serious hick town, where my dad served as pastor. Now I pastor in Walla Walla, Washington, another country town where the preacher says, "Bubba, could you pick up the offering?" and ten people stand who answer to the name "Bubba"—all of them women. Then they collect the offering with hubcaps. I'm proud to claim a hick town as where I come from. Everybody has a quick answer and a story when it comes to their birthplace.

But now for a stickier question: *Why* were you born? You can't get this answer from a birth certificate. An alarm clock can tell you *when* it's time to get up in the morning, but it won't tell you *why* you should get out of bed. *Why* were you born?

THE REAL QUESTION: WHAT'S IN THE BOX?

Bob Buford is a very successful businessman who tells of getting slammed by that question—*Why was I born?* He was extremely wealthy, the owner of a successful cable TV company. He lived in a mansion, drove a Jaguar, and taught a Sunday School class, but he didn't have a good answer to the question, "Why was I born?" He wondered, *What am I supposed to be doing here on earth? Is this it? Or is there a grander purpose in life?*

While wrestling with such questions, Buford hired a strategic planning consultant, Mike Kami. Mike had a brilliant mind with a stellar reputation in the highest echelons of the business community. After a couple hours of conversation, Mike drew a box on a sheet of paper and then asked Bob, "What's in the box?"

Bob was confused, so Mike told him about working with executives at Coca-Cola. When he led them through the same exercise, they put "taste" in the box. The most important thing to Coca-Cola was "taste," so that's what occupied the box. This led to the introduction of New Coke. Remember that? It was a disaster. The fiasco with New Coke sent the brass back to the box. They replaced "taste" with "American tradition." Tradition, they decided, should occupy the box. This led to the marketing of Classic Coke.

So once again, Mike pressed Bob with the question: "What's in your box?" Mike explained, "I can't put together an honest plan for your life until I identify the mainspring. I've been listening to you for a couple of hours, trying to figure out what's in your box. It's either money or Jesus Christ. If you can tell me which one it is, I can tell you the strategic-planning implications of that choice. If you can't tell me, you're going to bounce between those two values and be confused."

Bob writes, "No one had ever put such a significant question to me so directly. And he was exactly right. I was highly motivated to serve Jesus, but I also was driven to be financially successful. I believed the two went hand in hand, and in a way they do. But the reason I had such an unsettled feeling deep within was that I had tried to put two things in my 'box.'

"After a few minutes (which seemed like hours), I answered, 'Well, if it has to be one or the other, I'll put Jesus Christ in the box.'"[1]

Study the story of almost anyone and you'll quickly discern what's in their box. For Donald Trump, it's money. For Tiger Woods? A golf ball. For Imelda Marcos? It's a shoe box.

Bob Buford concludes his article by saying, "I can't tell you what to put in your box, but I can assure you that sooner or later you will choose. Your life will begin to race toward the one thing that is most important to you."[2]

So, what is in your box? Throughout human history people have put various things in the box.

THE QUESTER'S BOX

The Bible includes the journal of a man who anguished over this matter. In *The Message* translation, this man is referred to as "the Quester." What we often refer to as the book of Ecclesiastes, Eugene Peterson labels as "the words of the Quester" (Ecclesiastes 1:1, *The Message*). The author of Ecclesiastes is on a quest to find out what belongs in the box. Ecclesiastes is a window into the soul of a man who anguishes over the question, "Why am I here?"

I like the overview of Ecclesiastes that Pastor Mark Driscoll offers on the Mars Hill Fellowship Web site. This is his summary:

Pleasure 2:1—Solomon begins his search for meaning in life apart from God with the good times listed below.

Partying 2:3—Like a rich frat guy on a forty-year spring break, he drank good wine and lots of it.

Real Estate 2:4—He bought land, undertook construction projects, took seven years to build God's home and thirteen years to build his own, and also loved architecture and interior design.

Leisure 2:7—He had an army of servants to cater to his every whim, and this entourage was likely around thirty-five thousand people (see 1 Kings 4:22–23).

Wealth 2:8—From taxes alone, he earned twenty-five tons of gold in addition to the gold and exotic treasures brought by fleets of ships, accompanied by his innumerable other investments and income streams.

Music 2:8—Without our technological toys, Solomon had to hire professional musicians to follow him around, thus guaranteeing a soundtrack for his life.

Sex 2:8—If his seven hundred wives did not provide enough sexual variety, his three hundred concubines would have.

Conclusion 2:11—Solomon arranged every aspect of his external world so as to afford him maximum pleasure, but he never experienced enduring happiness and satisfaction because his internal condition remained sinful, and the highs of life experience eventually fade.[3]

"I DEVOTED MYSELF . . ."

I've always identified with Solomon, the author of Ecclesiastes, because he was an extremist. Over and over Solomon says, "I devoted myself . . ." to such and such a pursuit—and he did! He pursued these things with unbridled passion.

My family members all claim that I am an extremist, and I suppose it's true. For example, after we moved to Walla Walla,

someone served up some freshly picked, barbecued asparagus. They sprinkled it with olive oil, salt, and a little lemon,
and I thought I was at the feast in heaven. So the next Sunday
I decided to put up some barbecued asparagus for the winter.
A friend and I worked on it all day long, and by the end of the
day over half the freezer was stuffed with 75 pounds of asparagus. Years later, I still have 74.9999 pounds of frozen asparagus. As it turns out, it's not that good frozen. But after all
that work I can't just throw it away. With me, it's either 75
pounds or nothing. I tend to take everything to the extreme.

Solomon was like that. In his quest to figure out what belongs in the box, he relentlessly pursued many different ave-
nues. Let's consider three of his pursuits.

First, Solomon figured that wisdom was what belonged in
the box. He writes, "I devoted myself to study and to explore
by wisdom all that is done under heaven" (Ecclesiastes 1:13).
When Solomon tells us that he "devoted" himself to the pursuit of wisdom, he really did. He took this quest to the extreme. The Bible describes it like this: "God gave Solomon
wisdom and very great insight, and a breadth of understanding as measureless as the sand on the seashore. Solomon's
wisdom was greater than the wisdom of all the men of the
East, and greater than all the wisdom of Egypt. He was wiser
than any other man, including Ethan the Ezrahite—wiser
than Heman, Calcol and Darda, the sons of Mahol" (1 Kings
4:29–31).

Solomon was so smart that when a head of state paid him a
visit and grilled him with hard questions, the Bible records
that when "the queen of Sheba experienced for herself Solomon's wisdom . . . it took her breath away (1 Kings 10:4, 5, *The
Message*). Her response to all this was, "How happy your men
must be! How happy your officials, who continually stand before you and hear your wisdom!" (verse 8).

When was the last time someone fussed over you saying, "How lucky your family is to be around you and harvest the words of wisdom that drip from your lips! Your knowledge takes my breath away"?

Solomon was the smartest man who ever lived. He took brains to the extreme—only to discover the futility of wisdom. Wisdom can be overrated, as the following story illustrates.

In 1996, Oklahoma State University had a sorry football team. The quarterback, Randy Johnson (the nephew of former U.S. President Lyndon Johnson), lacked the skills to salvage a sorry season. But the players could still enjoy legendary status if they beat their main rival, the University of Oklahoma, in the final game of the season.

But things didn't look good. With only seconds remaining on the clock, Oklahoma State found themselves on their own twenty-yard line and trailing by six points.

As a gesture of goodwill, the Oklahoma State coach put in all the seniors for the last play of the game and told Randy to call whatever play he wanted. To everyone's surprise, Randy called play thirteen—a trick play the team had never used because it had never worked in practice.

Well, the miracle happened! Play thirteen worked! Oklahoma State scored! Randy Johnson's team won the game! The players hoisted Randy on their shoulders and triumphantly carried him off the field.

When the coach cornered Randy after the game, he had to know. "Why in the world did you ever call play thirteen?"

"Well, we were in the huddle," Randy answered, "and I looked over and saw old Harry with tears running down his cheeks. It was his last college game, and we were losing. And I saw that big eight on his chest. Then I looked over and saw Ralph. Tears were running down his cheeks, too. And I saw that big seven on his jersey. So in honor of those two heartbroken seniors, I added eight and seven together and called play thirteen!"

"But Randy," the coach replied, "eight and seven don't add up to thirteen!"

Randy reflected for a moment and answered, "You're right, coach. And if I'd been as smart as you are, we would have lost the game!"[4]

You can put brains in your box if you'd like, but sometimes being smart is overrated. You can have more degrees than a thermometer and still manage to have a miserable and messed-up life—because wisdom is not a wise thing to put in your box.

The Quester learned as much, so he opted to place pleasure in the box. And again, he took pleasure to the extreme. Ecclesiastes 2:1 records, "I thought in my heart, 'Come now, I will test you with pleasure to find out what is good.' But that also proved to be meaningless."

The Quester pursues pleasure but discovers only emptiness there. Actress Winona Ryder tells of her pursuit of pleasure and finally cracking into elite circles of Hollywood—that pleasure palace. She learned quickly, however, that life in Hollywood can be onion-skin shallow. Winona writes, "When I was 18, I was driving around at two in the morning, completely crying and alone and scared. I drove by this magazine stand that had this *Rolling Stone* [magazine] that I was on the cover of, and it said, 'Winona Ryder: The Luckiest Girl in the World.' And there I was feeling more alone than I ever had."[5] Like the Quester of old, Winona discovered the pointlessness of pursuing pleasure.

The Quester left no stone unturned in his pursuit of pleasure. "I tried cheering myself with wine," he writes (Ecclesiastes 2:3). A lot of people look for pleasure in the bottle but land on skid row.

Then he thinks that maybe sexual pleasure is the key to his satisfaction. So he rides that avenue to the extreme. Scripture records that Solomon had one thousand wives and concubines. And this is the smartest guy in the world?

The Quester then proclaims, "I denied myself nothing my eyes desired; I refused my heart no pleasure" (Ecclesiastes 2:10). But it wasn't enough. So he recklessly throws himself into another pursuit: success. He writes: "I undertook great projects" (verse 4). He goes on to describe building gardens and parks, amassing possessions and fame.

Solomon tasted the heady harvest of success. He extended his country's borders beyond the boundaries achieved by any king of Israel before or since. He masterminded an unparalleled economic boom. He redefined leadership success.

We're told that "the weight of the gold that Solomon received yearly was 666 talents" (1 Kings 10:14)—or about twenty-five tons. Imagine: Every year, in addition to taxes and profits from trades, Solomon received twenty-five tons of gold! In today's dollars that would convert to a base salary of roughly $340 million—or $93,000 a day!

"King Solomon was greater in riches and wisdom than all the other kings of the earth. The whole world sought audience with Solomon" (1 Kings 10:23, 24). At different seasons of his life, Solomon put wisdom and pleasure and success in the box—and each one turned out like the introduction of New Coke, a great disappointment. His quest brought him full circle back to some of the most basic questions of life: Why was I born? What is life all about?

THE QUESTER'S ANSWER

Toward the end of the Quester's journal he penned this entry: "Remember your Creator in the days of your youth, before the days of trouble come" (Ecclesiastes 12:1). Here is the only answer that makes any sense. A life spent with God is the only life that has meaning.

Charles Swindoll points out that the Hebrew word translated *remember* in this verse means "to act decisively on behalf of someone."[6] Solomon is saying, "act decisively" for God. In other words, be intentional. Cheat the lesser gods that clamor for your affections in order to honor the one and only true God. "Do this," Solomon urges, "while you are still young, before the days of trouble come."

He then offers some colorful images that capture the angst of aging:

- "When the grinders cease because they are few" (Ecclesiastes 12:3). The "grinders" refer to the teeth. They start falling out!
- "And those looking through the windows grow dim" (verse 3). In other words our eyesight starts to fade. The windows get cloudy.
- "When men rise at the sound of birds, but all their songs grow faint" (verse 4). As you age, it gets harder to sleep at night. Birds wake you up, but you can't hear them very well because your hearing is almost gone!
- "When the almond tree blossoms" (verse 5). This is a picture of graying hair. Have you ever seen an almond tree in full bloom? It shimmers in silver and gray.
- And "the grasshopper drags himself along" (verse 5). The "get up and go" is gone; the grasshopper has lost its hop.
- And then Solomon writes at the end, and "desire is no longer stirred" (verse 5).

Maybe you're young now, the Quester says, but some day the grinders are going to rot, the windows will get cloudy, the chirping of the birds will be difficult to hear, the grasshopper's going to lose its gumption, and then the mourners will cry for a few minutes before they retreat to the fellowship hall and chow down on potato salad.

So what is the point of life? Maybe Mark Twain was right when he wrote shortly before he died: "A myriad of men are born; they labor and sweat and struggle; . . . they squabble and scold and fight; they scramble for little mean advantages over each other; age creeps upon them; infirmities follow; . . . those they love are taken from them, and the joy of life is turned to aching grief. [Death] comes at last—the only unpoisoned gift earth ever had for them—and they vanish from a world where they were of no consequence, . . . a world which will lament them a day and forget them forever."[7]

Is that the point of life? To live so the world will lament your passing for a day and then forget you forever?

Solomon would argue "No!" Instead he concludes with this sobering challenge: "Now all has been heard; here is the conclusion of the matter: Fear God and keep his commandments, for this is the whole duty of man" (Ecclesiastes 12:13).

Boil it down and herein lies the meaning of life: We're called to fear God. That's why you and I were born. Apart from God, life is meaningless. Cheat God, and you will cheat yourself of life.

Solomon's warning rings clear: Now is your time to strengthen the connection between you and God. Before it's too late, figure out what goes in your box. Put anything other than God in your box, and you are destined for a life of futility.

A well-worn children's story helps to illustrate. As the story goes, a spider dropped a single strand down from the rafter of an old barn and began to weave his web. Day by day the spider stretched his web until it spanned an expansive fly zone. Daily the web snagged a buffet of bugs, making the spider the envy of all spiders.

One day, the spider was cruising along his elaborately woven web and noticed the single strand disappearing into the rafters. *Hmmm*, the spider wondered, *of what value is that strand? It's not going to catch me my dinner.* With that thought the spider climbed up . . . and severed the single strand. Of course, the entire web swallowed the spider as he floated downward to his demise.[8]

Like the spider, Solomon learned the hard way what happens when you sever the strand that connects you to God *above the sun.* He searched for meaning in a life lived *under the sun.* In fact, that phrase "under the sun" occurs twenty-nine times in the book of Ecclesiastes. It describes Solomon's quest for meaning by looking for wisdom and pleasure and success *under the sun.* In the end, however, he concludes that life has no meaning apart from God.

That's the message of the Quester to sophisticated postmoderns who clamor for an answer to the question "Why am I here?"

Why? To find and to know God.[9] As Augustine put it, "He who has God has everything. He who does not have God has nothing. He who has God and everything has no more than he who has God alone."[10]

Answering Life's Biggest Questions
(Questions for Reflection or Group Study)

1. When were you born? Where were you born? Why were you born?
2. Do you remember when Coke introduced New Coke? Why do you think it bombed?
3. The Quester tried putting wisdom, pleasure, and success in his box. What other things do people try putting in the box? Have you ever been on a quest for something that you later saw as futile?

4. Is there any area in your life in which you can relate to being an extremist like the Quester? Share an example.
5. If God approached you, as He did Solomon, and offered you anything, what would you ask for?
6. In the book of Proverbs, wisdom is described as being more valuable than silver or gold. Given the opportunity to live life over with more wisdom, what would you do differently?
7. Have you ever been disillusioned in the pursuit of pleasure? If so, why do you think you were disappointed?
8. What does success look like for you?
9. Share five ways that you can find and know God today. Put your suggestions into practice this week.
10. What will you put in your box?

1. Bob Buford, "Don't be Miserable," <http://www.oldmannewman.com/onlineextras/chapters/5/miserable.html>.

2. Ibid.

3. Adapted from <http://lite.marshillchurch.org/index.php?section_id=b35bb9687c96-4990-b744-fc34390sabd8&id=9ee7f272-88a1-493b-af28-05c3f7a1dd61>.

4. Wayne Rice, ed., *Still More Hot Illustrations for Youth Talks* (Grand Rapids, Mich.: Zondervan Publishing House, 1999), pp. 31, 32.

5. Winona Ryder, cited from *Plugged In,* vol. 6, no. 4 (April, 2001).

6. Charles Swindoll, *Living on the Ragged Edge* (Dallas: Word Publishing, 1985), p. 349.

7. <http://www.sermonillustrations.com/a-z/t/twain_mark.htm>.

8. Max Lucado, *Turn #1 Toward God's Glory* (Portland, Ore.: Multnomah Publishers, 2005).

9. Larry L. Lichtenwalter, *Well Driven Nails* (Hagerstown, Md.: Review and Herald Publishing Association, 1999), p. 22.

10. <http://lite.marshillchurch.org/index.php?section_id=b35bb9687c96-4990-b744-fc34390sabd8&id=9ee7f272-88a1-493b-af28-05c3f7a1dd61>.

—Chapter two—
Speed or Soul?

We are a nation obsessed with hurry. We're the only country in the world that has a national monument called Mount Rushmore!

On a flight recently I was reminded of this obsession with rushing around. I noticed that there was a fly in the airplane. Guess what the fly was doing. It was *flying!* And I wondered, *Why would a fly in a plane, fly in a plane?*

Have you ever felt like that fly? Do you ever feel like you're living in a world that is flying six hundred miles an hour and in the middle of all the chaos you're flying just as fast? James Thurber writes, "Man is flying too fast for a world that is round. Soon he will catch up with himself in a great rear-end collision, and man will never know that what hit him from behind was man."[1] That's how fast we're moving these days.

THE "SPEED VS. SOUL" EQUATION

You can get sucked into the world's insane hurricane of activity and busyness, but when you do, your soul is in peril. Get swept away by the speed of life, and you will sabotage your soul.

Pastor Bill Hybels describes the danger in this way:

> If you don't care much about your soul, if you don't care much that your soul is dry and arid and barren and dying, if you don't care much that your soul is not responsive to God and doesn't feel his presence and

power and favor and delight in your life, if you don't care much about having soulful connections with other people—keep your foot on the accelerator and mash it to the firewall. . . .

But if your soul matters to you, if you generally like feeling human, if you generally like being more than a machine, then you've got to adjust the speed versus soul equation in your life.[2]

In that same sermon Hybels talked about his regular visits to Harvard Business School to dialogue with students about an ongoing case study that the university has done on the church that Hybels started. Toward the end of the class one student raised his hand and said that although he wasn't a religious person, he wondered if Hybels had any pastoral counsel for them as they were getting ready to graduate. Listen to Hybels's response:

"You're going to go out, and you're going to be recruited and hired into some high velocity companies, and they're going to pay you a lot of money to keep charts going up and to the right, and if you're not careful you're going to become a commerce machine. You're going to lose touch with your soul.

"And 10 or 15 years from now, nobody's going to know you. You might have gone through a couple of marriages; you might have some kids who wonder where their dad or their mom is. I would just ask you to guard your soul. Keep it alive."[3]

The class sat like statues. Hybels said it was as if half the class were saying, "I think I've already lost my soul. I think it's happened already. I feel like a machine now."

THE SOUL AND SCRIPTURE

The world may be stuck on fast-forward, but you don't have to be. This is what Scripture teaches.

Listen to the invitation that Jesus offered people who were worn out, burned out, and stressed out. He said, " 'Come to me, all you who are weary and burdened, and I will give you rest. Take my yoke upon you and learn from me, for I am gentle and humble in heart, and you will find rest for your souls' " (Matthew 11:28, 29).

"Rest for your soul." That sounds inviting, doesn't it? It's possible. How? You must live intimately connected with Christ.

This metaphor of the yoke is foreign to us today because John Deere came along and made yokes obsolete. But in Jesus' culture this word picture would have immediately connected with His audience. A yoke, of course, is a type of harness that connects a pair of oxen. In those days, a pair of oxen was actually called a "yoke" of oxen. Moreover, in Jesus' day, a yoke was often used metaphorically to refer to submission to a teacher. Rabbis used the phrase "to take the yoke of . . ." to speak of becoming a committed pupil of a particular teacher.

It's no secret that over the years I have been heavily influenced in my spiritual journey by Pastor John Ortberg. He doesn't know it, but in many respects I have yoked up with him in ministry. What does this mean? It means that I have been his devoted student. I have hundreds of his sermon tapes. I have dozens of his sermon manuscripts. I have read all of his books several times. I have heard him preach at conferences and at his church on numerous occasions. I have learned a great deal from him about how to do life with God. Much of what I teach and write is heavily influenced by my favorite teacher, John Ortberg.

That's the kind of invitation that Jesus offers to you: "Take My yoke upon you, and learn from Me." J. H. Jowett, the nineteenth-century English Congregationalist, put it like this:

"A yoke is a neck harness for two, and the Lord Himself pleads to be One of the two. He wants to share the labor of any galling task. The secret of peace and victory in the Christian life is found in putting off the taxing collar of 'self' and accepting the Master's relaxing 'yoke.' "[4]

Another text in Scripture that informs our understanding of how to find rest for the soul is Isaiah 26:3. I still prefer the old King James Version for this text: "Thou wilt keep him in perfect peace, whose mind is stayed on thee."

Harrison Ford, the well-known actor whose movies have grossed more than two billion dollars, once quipped, "You only want what you ain't got."

A reporter then asked, "Well, what ain't you got?"

Ford answered with one word: "Peace."[5]

The Bible promises that you can experience *perfect* peace. How? By keeping your focus fixed on God.

Consider one more text that enlightens our understanding of how to live our lives toward the "soul" side rather than the "speed" side. Jesus taught, " 'So do not worry, saying, "What shall we eat?" or "What shall we drink?" or "What shall we wear?" For the pagans run after all these things, and your heavenly Father knows that you need them. But seek first his kingdom and his righteousness, and all these things will be given to you as well' " (Matthew 6:31–33).

Jesus looked at the pagans racing like greyhounds to get ahead. They stressed over such things as what to wear and what to eat. Jesus reminds us that we don't have to live like that. Our souls can be at rest by living in the presence of Jesus. We really can trust all these matters to God.

Some years ago I heard the story of a speedboat driver racing along at near top speed when a bad combination of wind and waves catapulted him high into the air, spinning crazily. He was thrown from his boat and thrust deeply into the water—so deep, in fact, that he did not know which way was up. Frantically, he kicked and thrashed and panicked . . . until it dawned on him that he was wearing a life vest. When he stopped fighting, the buoyancy of the life vest reoriented him so he could swim toward the surface.

Next time you're flying through life and find yourself so deeply immersed in your worries that you don't know which way is up, just stop. Remind yourself to trust God and seek first His kingdom. Allow God's gentle tug to pull you in the proper direction. No need to panic. Step out of the speed cycle and nurture your soul.

VOCABULARY OF THE SOUL

So now it's time to decide. There is an inverse relationship between speed and soul. You invest yourself in one only at the expense of the other. You can't nurture a healthy soul on the run.

Chances are, this sounds great to you, but to pull it off in real life you will need to become a master at saying certain things. You'll need to practice the very earthy vocabulary of the soul. Repeat these phrases over and over if you are to carve out room for your soul.

The first phrase is one word: "No!" One of the reasons we are so busy is that we just can't stomach the thought of missing the chance to score some points at work or make an extra wad of cash or take a trip. We're opportunity junkies that keep cramming more and more activity into limited space. We feel guilty if we don't capitalize on every break that comes along.

If you're going to get a handle on the speed factor of life, you must become a master at saying this word: "No!" It's a great word. It's one of the first words we learn as human beings. When my daughter was two years old, she would emphatically screech "No!" if I asked her about anything!

"Will you eat your broccoli?"

"No!"

"Will you pick up your toys?"

"No!"

"Will you ever borrow dad's car?"

"No!" (I will remind her of that conversation in a few years.)

But we never outgrow the usefulness of that word. Perhaps you need to exercise your "No" muscle.

"Will you stay at the office a couple extra hours to finish the project?"

"Will you come over and watch the ball game with the guys?"

"Will you take getting bumped from a flight even though it means an extra night away from the family?"

Practice saying it today: "No."

Another helpful phrase in your soul vocabulary is, "You win!" Remember, you can't win at everything. When I drive through our neighborhood at Christmas time and see all the homes decked out with lights, I roll down my windows and shout "You win!" I'm not going to clutter my life by competing in contests such as Christmas lights, making money, book sales, number of articles published, the best sermons preached—the list just goes on and on. And to give my soul some space to grow, I find myself resigning myself to the fact that I cannot compete in every arena. So you have to decide where you want to excel and where you're going to surrender—and just say, "You win." Recognize that some opportunities will simply need to be left behind.

The final statement that I find helpful for growing a healthy soul is a simple prayer: "God, I resign as ruler of the universe." This is a way of reminding myself not to worry about a lot of things I cannot control. Rather, I will simply trust God to run the world. I don't have to try and control my kids or my wife or my colleagues at work; I just have to trust God, moment by moment. When you really begin to live in this daily intimacy with God, trusting Him in all matters, life becomes an incredible adventure. Your soul flourishes with the abundance of everything that is genuinely good.

Take, for example, the story of Dr. George McCauslin. He was hailed as one of the greatest YMCA directors of all time. He served at a troubled YMCA near Pittsburgh. The club had perennial problems: declining memberships, financial difficulties, and challenging staff issues. McCauslin found himself working eighty-five hours a week and getting little sleep at night. Whenever he tried to take time off, he just worried all the more about the problems at work.

McCauslin went to a therapist, who told him he was on the verge of a nervous breakdown. He had to learn to release his worries. But how?

He took an afternoon off, escaping to the woods of western Pennsylvania. As McCauslin walked through the cool woods, he could feel his tight body start to relax. He sat down under a tree and sighed. For the first time in months he relaxed.

Finding a pen and pad of paper in his coat, he wrote this letter to God: "Dear God, today I hereby resign as general manager of the universe. Love, George."

McCauslin later told a friend: "And wonder of wonders, God accepted my resignation."[6]

And He will accept yours, too, if you completely trust Him.

Your soul matters. Jesus asked, "What does it profit a person to gain the whole world and lose his own soul?" (see Mark 8:36). What good is it, if you're CEO of a Fortune 500 company, a Pulitzer Prize winner, the first chair in the city orchestra, a scratch handicapper at the country club, and the head deacon of your church—if you lose your soul? You don't want to go there. So guard your soul.

Perhaps you want to expand this list of phrases that safeguard the soul. Put the list in a prominent place so you can be reminded regularly of things you must say in order to shield yourself from soul fatigue. No one will do this for you. Your boss, your kids, your spouse, your neighbors—everyone screams for a piece of you. So you must choose to align your life with *your* values. You can do this by regularly practicing a vocabulary that builds boundaries around your soul.

Speed or soul—you can't do both. Speed is the number one enemy of spiritual life. Your soul must have ample space and ample time to grow in God. It's time to decide.

Speed or Soul?
(Questions for Reflection or Group Study)

1. On a continuum of the speed versus soul equation, with one being 100 percent speed and ten being 100 percent soul, where would you currently put yourself? Why? Would you like to change your position on the continuum?
2. What counsel would you have for Harvard graduates itching to make their mark on the world?
3. Rewrite the texts (Matthew 11:28, 29; Isaiah 26:3; Matthew 6:31–33) from this chapter using contemporary language.
4. What does it mean to you to wear the yoke of Jesus?
5. Has your soul ever felt at perfect peace? If so, when?
6. What do you worry about the most? How can you release those worries to Jesus?
7. Describe situations that cause you to push the panic button.

8. Meyer Friedman, M.D., claims that hurry sickness destroys people physically and spiritually. Have you seen symptoms of this disease in your life? Describe them. Using the texts in this chapter, write a prescription for yourself.

9. Expand your vocabulary of the soul. What other statements must you make regularly to manage the speed factor in your life? What character qualities do you hope to grow as a result of this study?

---

1. Quoted by Phil Callaway, *Who Put My Life on Fast-Forward?* (Eugene, Ore.: Harvest House Publishers, 2002), p. 9.

2. Bill Hybels, "I Have a Friend Who . . . Struggles With Balancing Life's Demands," Sermon preached March 25, 2001, at Willow Creek Community Church, South Barrington, Illinois, p. 8.

3. Ibid., p. 6.

4. Quoted on <http://sermoncentral.com/print_friendly.asp?ContributorID=&SermonID=49844>, p. 3.

5. Ibid., p. 2.

6. Thomas Tewell, "The Weight of the World [1995]," *Preaching Today,* tape no. 147, cited at <http://preachingtoday.com/index.taf?_UserReference=72F728A021191C4342F7D147&_function=illustration&_op=show_pf&IID=4769&sr=1>.

Chapter three

How Much Faith
Do You Need?

Whenever I'm in the mood to just laugh, I pop in my favorite video. I've watched it at least fifty times, and it still cracks me up. I've played it at churches and conferences all around the world—delighting thousands of people over the years.

It's a video of my brother, Paul, challenging his neighbor to a race. My brother is a running wannabe. His neighbor, Phillimon Hanneck, is the real deal. Hanneck competed as a runner, representing Zimbabwe, at the Olympic Games in 1992 and continues to compete professionally now as an American citizen. So my brother challenged him to a race, and we had a video camera rolling.

Before Phillimon arrives, Paul rambles for the camera: "It's an early morning out here where I occasionally like to jog on the golf course," he says. "Yesterday I ran into a neighbor, and I challenged him to a foot race. He seems to have done a little running—like myself."

The video then cuts to a clip of Phillimon Hanneck competing (as the sports announcer explains) in his "eloquent three minute, fifty-three second-mile form."

Back to Paul: "It's really only fair to mention that I liked to run when I was back in high school at Laurelwood Academy in Gaston, Oregon. We didn't have a track program as such; in fact, we didn't even have a track. But we did have a field, and I liked to run in the field. I was pretty fast running around the field—I just wanted to mention that in fairness to my competitor today. I do have experience in running. It wasn't a big school; there were about three hundred students. But of the three hundred, I was certainly one of them."

At last Phillimon arrives, and Paul explains that they will run to an umbrella he has stuck in the ground about a hundred yards away, turn around it, and come back to finish at the starting line. The starting gun fires, and both men gallop away. In spite of Paul's herculean efforts (he even cheats by turning around twenty yards in front of the umbrella), Phillimon blows by him on the final stretch to take the checkered flag. Paul is panting while Phillimon looks cool and collected, like he's ready to dine with the president.

Here's the deal with Phillimon Hanneck: I admire him; I just can't relate to him. Every day he jogs sixteen miles and does two hours of yoga and two hours of weight training. He told my brother, "I never put anything into my mouth that doesn't help me win the next race." He no longer lives next to my brother because he moved to a house that, as I understand it, is oxygen-controlled so it's the equivalent of living at the same altitude as Colorado—except that he still gets to live in Portland where it rains all the time.

I admire Phillimon Hanneck, but I can't relate to him. I relate to my brother, his fat flapping in the wind and threatening to burst open the Spandex. That's me—racing as fast as I can, but next to a real athlete I'm a joke.

OLYMPIC SAINTS

Spiritually speaking, I feel the same way at times. Scripture is loaded with stories of saints who demonstrated Olympic-size faith. I admire these people in the Bible; I just can't relate to them.

For example, one time a Roman centurion approached Jesus and asked Him to heal his servant. Jesus replied, "OK, I'll come to your house and heal him."

"You don't need to come to my house," the centurion objected. "All You have to do is say the word."

The Bible records, "When Jesus heard this, he was astonished and said to those following him, 'I tell you the truth, I have not found anyone in Israel with such great faith.' . . . 'Go! It will be done just as you believed it would.' And his servant was healed at that very hour" (Matthew 8:10, 13).

Now that's Olympic-size faith!

Mark 10 preserves the story of Bartimaeus, a blind beggar in Jericho. When Jesus came to town, Bartimaeus started screaming, "Jesus, Son of David, have mercy on me."

The crowd tried to hush him, but he wouldn't shut up because his faith was so strong. Jesus asked him what he wanted, and he said, "I want to see."

" 'Go,' said Jesus, 'your faith has healed you.' Immediately he received his sight and followed Jesus along the road" (Mark 10:52).

That's Olympic-size faith!

Then there is a story in Mark 5 in which a multitude of people are pressing in on Jesus. A woman who has been bleeding for twelve years touches His garment. The text tells us that she had suffered a great deal under the care of many doctors and had spent all she had trying to find healing. But the woman believes that if she can just touch the hem of His garment, she'll be healed. And she was.

We pick up the story in verse 30:

At once Jesus realized that power had gone out from him. He turned around in the crowd and asked, "Who touched my clothes?"

"You see the people crowding against you," his disciples answered, "and yet you can ask, 'Who touched me?' "

But Jesus kept looking around to see who had done it. Then the woman, knowing what had happened to her, came and fell at his feet and, trembling with fear, told him the whole truth. He said to her, "Daughter, your faith has healed you. Go in peace and be freed from your suffering."

THAT'S OLYMPIC-SIZE FAITH!

The Bible is packed with stories of people who are spiritual Olympians. I admire them; I just can't relate.

When I read Bible stories like that, I feel like the students who ended up with a substitute teacher for the day. The substitute teacher had injured his back and had to wear a plaster cast around the upper part of his body, but it wasn't noticeable under his shirt. It happened that the students this teacher was assigned to for the day were the toughest students in the school. This class had a reputation across the county as being the most unruly and misbehaved kids you'd ever find.

Striding confidently into the rowdy classroom, the teacher opened the window as wide as possible and then busied himself with desk work. When a strong breeze made his tie flap, he took the desk stapler and (making sure all the kids in the classroom were watching) *stapled the tie to his chest!*

Discipline wasn't a problem all day long! The students saw that teacher as a superhero.

Well, that's how I see these people in the Bible who cause Jesus to marvel at their faith. They're spiritual superheroes, and I'll never be like them. Which begs the question: How much faith do I need?

The answer comes from a guy in the New Testament that is no spiritual Olympian. He's an Olympic wannabe, but this guy is no player at all.

AN OLYMPIC WANNABE

A man in the crowd answered, "Teacher, I brought you my son, who is possessed by a spirit that has robbed him of speech. Whenever it seizes him, it throws him to the ground. He foams at the mouth, gnashes his teeth and becomes rigid. I asked your disciples to drive out the spirit, but they could not."

"O unbelieving generation," Jesus replied, "how long shall I stay with you? How long shall I put up with you? Bring the boy to me" (Mark 9:17–19).

Max Lucado offers this commentary: "Where is the faith in this picture? The disciples have failed, the scribes are amused, the demon is victorious, and the father is desperate. You'd be hard-pressed to find a needle of belief in that haystack."[1]

The story continues:

So they brought him. When the spirit saw Jesus, it immediately threw the boy into a convulsion. He fell to the ground and rolled around, foaming at the mouth.

Jesus asked the boy's father, "How long has he been like this?"

"From childhood," he answered. "It has often thrown him into fire or water to kill him. But if you can do anything, take pity on us and help us" (Mark 9:20–22).

Out of the din of doubt comes this timid request, "If You can . . ."

That's a pretty puny prayer, isn't it? You're not likely to hear that kind of prayer in church: "Dear heavenly Father, if You can do anything . . ."

You won't find the phrase in any great hymn: "Joyful, joyful, we adore Thee, if You can, if You can . . ."

"If you can"? said Jesus. "Everything is possible for him who believes."

Immediately the boy's father exclaimed, "I do believe; help me overcome my unbelief!" (Mark 9:23, 24).

Notice that Mark says the father replies "immediately." That's how close his disbelief is to the surface. "That's my problem," the man admits at once. "I don't have much faith. Help my unbelief."

Now things get real quiet. The disciples are probably wondering, *We've never seen anybody try this approach before. How is Jesus going to respond to this spiritual weakling?* "When Jesus saw that a crowd was running to the scene, he rebuked the evil spirit. 'You deaf and mute spirit,' he said, 'I command you, come out of him and never enter him again' " (Mark 9:25).

Shocking, don't you think? The man has admitted that he doesn't have enough faith to believe that Jesus can pull it off. And how does Jesus respond? He heals the boy.

Apparently, Jesus prefers honesty to certainty. That's why Jesus warned us not to babble on mindlessly in our prayers, uttering pious sounding clichés. God wants us just to be real rather than really spiritual sounding.

Think about how easy it is for our prayers to deteriorate into a mindless recitation of spiritual sounding clichés. I sit down to a meal of deep-fried fat that's slathered in butter and covered with sugar. And what do I pray? "Dear God, bless this food to the nourishment of my body." If I'm sincere about this prayer, then I ought to say, "Dear God, turn this Big Mac and Coke into tree bark and tofu." God is not amused with hypocritical, dishonest prayers.

Notice what happens after Jesus commands the demon to depart from the boy: "The spirit shrieked, convulsed him violently and came out. The boy looked so much like a corpse that many said, 'He's dead.' But Jesus took him by the hand and lifted him to his feet, and he stood up" (Mark 9:26, 27).

That's the Bible account. But let's imagine this story from the father's perspective.

When Benjamin was born we knew something was wrong. When he was a year old, I dropped a ceramic plate right next to him. It shattered, but my boy never flinched. Snapping my fingers next to his ears yielded the same result. We knew early on that he was a deaf mute. I would never hear my boy say, "I love you, Dad."

He was also an epileptic. We could never travel far from the hospital.

But even worse, Benjamin was demon-possessed. You understand this cast a lot of scorn on me, his father. People all over town murmured, wondering what sin I had committed to cause this curse upon my son.

Other dads took their boys to ball games. They bragged about how big and strong and fast their boys were. Benjamin was developmentally challenged. He was the one they made jokes about.

One time we tried to take Benjamin camping. That proved to be a disaster. I turned my back for just a moment and saw my boy sitting in the fire. I dragged him out and doused him with dirt. The next morning he nearly drowned in the lake near our campsite. There really was no reason to pretend that we were a normal family that took camping trips. It was a bleak situation. I was on alert twenty-four hours a day, seven days a week—desperate, hopeless, and exhausted.

Then I heard about this healer named Jesus. The stories sparked an ember of hope. Jesus had just been in the vicinity of the Decapolis where some people brought a deaf man who could hardly speak—and Jesus healed him. Then He fed four thousand people with seven loaves and a few small fishes. Then he healed a blind man at Bethsaida.

I figured it was all smoke and mirrors, but I was so desperate. So on the off chance that it was more than hype, I set out to track Him down. I happened onto His disciples and asked if they could heal my boy. "Of course," they assured me. "We have the power of God at our disposal. Bring him to us."

Hope surged within my soul. My heart raced, giddy with anticipation.

"Depart from him!" the disciples demanded of the demon. They slapped Benjamin's forehead. My heart stopped.

But nothing happened.

My boy was still locked in his prison of insanity. I should have known better. We all know the cliché, right? "If it sounds too good to be true, it probably is." I felt like an idiot for hoping.

Just then Jesus arrived on the scene. I was desperate. I threw myself at His feet and cried out, "Teacher, I brought my mute son, made speechless by a demon, to you. Whenever it seizes him, it throws him to the ground. He foams at the mouth, grinds his teeth, and goes stiff as a board. I told your disciples, hoping they could deliver him, but they couldn't" (Mark 9:17, 18, *The Message*).

Jesus didn't attempt to hide His disgust. He said, "What a generation! No sense of God! How many times do I have to go over these things? How much longer do I have to put up with this? Bring the boy here" (Mark 9:19, *The Message*).

I dragged Benjamin to Jesus. He groveled in the dirt and spit on Jesus. He cursed and kicked.

Jesus wanted to know how long he'd been like this. I said, "All his life." Then I begged Jesus, "If you can do anything, do it. Have a heart and help us!" (Mark 9:22, *The Message*).

Jesus was incredulous. "If?" He barked. "There are no 'ifs' among believers. Anything can happen" (Mark 9:23, *The Message*).

I cried out, "Then I believe. Help me with my doubts!"

Immediately Benjamin stopped his convulsions. At first I feared that he had died. But then he sat up. And for the first time in his life he looked me in the eye, and he said, "Dad?"

He recognized me! I threw my arms around him and repeated over and over, "I love you, son. I love you, son."

Max Lucado offers this commentary: "A parent with a sick son in need of a miracle. The father's prayer isn't much, but the answer is, and the result reminds us: The power is not in the prayer; it's in the one who hears it."[2]

Following this whole drama, the disciples cornered Jesus and asked Him privately, "Why couldn't we cast out the demon? What happened?"

Jesus answered, "That kind of a demon can only be exorcised by prayer."

No doubt the disciples prayed, but they believed the miracle was really about them. And their insincere prayers ricocheted off the ceiling. In reality, miracles are all about God. The power is not in the one who prays, but in the One who hears the prayer. Similarly, faith is not about some magic formula or a certain feeling of certainty. Faith is all about the One in whom we trust.

And since God is more concerned about our hurt than our eloquence, He honors the feeblest of faith. That's the heart of our Father.

AN OLYMPIC MOMENT

We see that same heart in Jim Redmond. His story takes us back to the same Olympics where Phillimon Hanneck competed—Barcelona, 1992. Jim's twenty-six-year-old son, Derek Redmond, was favored to win the four-hundred-meter race. He was the British runner who skyrocketed to fame by shattering his country's four-hundred-meter record at age nineteen. With only 175 meters left in the race, Derek was coasting to a victory when he ripped his hamstring. His leg quivering, he hopped on the left leg and then collapsed. Paramedics scurried to the scene, but Derek refused to get on the stretcher.

"It was animal instinct," Derek would later reflect. He limped onward in a crazed attempt to reach the finish line. On the homestretch, a big man parted the crowd surrounding Derek. His T-shirt asked, "Have you hugged your child today?" His hat commanded, "Just do it." The man was Derek's dad, Jim Redmond.

"You don't have to do this," he consoled his bawling boy.

"Yes, I do," Derek countered.

"Well, then," Jim said, "we're going to finish this together."

And they did. At times Derek buried his face in his father's shoulder. Together, arm in arm, father and son staggered toward the finish line as sixty-five thousand fans stood, clapped, then cried.

What made the father leave the stands to attend to his boy? Was it the strength of his son? No. It was his son's *weakness*. His child was in anguish, trying to finish the race, so the father vacated the stands to support him.

Our Father does the same. No matter how weak or insufficient you feel, no matter how splintered your soul, when you cry to God for help, He will abandon heaven to come to your side. You don't need a mountain of faith—just a mustard seed. Just enough faith to call on Jesus—that's all the faith you need.

How Much Faith Do You Need?
(Questions for Reflection or Group Study)

1. What athlete best represents your spiritual condition right now? Why?
2. On a spiritual continuum, with "one" being a pure Olympic wannabe and "ten" being a finely tuned, gold medal athlete, where would you put yourself? Why?
3. What is the one prayer right now that you would most like God to answer?
4. How do you react to stories of people in Scripture who demonstrated great faith?
5. What did Jesus mean in Mark 9:23 when He said, "Everything is possible for him who believes"?
6. Where in your life do you have the strongest faith? What are the barriers to faith in your life?
7. "I do believe; help me overcome my unbelief." Have you ever said that to God? When? Is this a confession of faith or doubt?
8. Discuss other stories in the Bible where God honored weakness.
9. Pray a prayer that stretches your faith.

---

1. Max Lucado, *He Still Moves Stones* (Dallas: Word Publishing, 1993), p. 100.
2. Ibid., p. 98.

—Section 2—
Soul Pain

"A wretched soul,

bruised with adversity,

We bid be quiet when we hear it cry;

But were we burdened

with like weight of pain,

As much, or more,

we should ourselves complain."

(William Shakespeare, 1564–1616)

—Chapter four—
Siegfried and Roy
and Our Untamable God

In 1957, Siegfried and Roy met on a German cruise ship, where Siegfried worked as a steward and Roy as a waiter. They soon discovered they shared a number of things in common. They were both raised by abusive, alcoholic fathers. Both of their dads had served in Hitler's Nazi army. And, of course, they shared a love of magic.

One night, while horsing around on a makeshift stage, Roy saw Siegfried pull a rabbit out of a hat. Roy asked him if he could do the same illusion using a cheetah. (Roy had smuggled on board his pet cheetah named Chico.) Siegfried assured him that he could, and as they say, the rest is history.

For thirty years this dynamic duo dominated the strip in Las Vegas, the entertainment capital of the world, delighting over twenty-five million show-goers. After five thousand shows using wild animals without incident, the unthinkable happened. On Friday, October 3, 2003 (Roy Horn's fifty-ninth birthday), a seven-year-old, six-hundred-pound royal white tiger named Montecore grabbed Roy by the neck and carried him offstage. Backstage, show attendants doused the cat with fire extinguishers—but not before a lot of damage had been done. Roy is very fortunate to be alive.

Siegfried was quick to defend the tiger, suggesting that Montecore accidentally mauled Roy. Later he tried to get the tiger off the hook by explaining that the animal had been trying to help Horn after the illusionist slipped during the performance. More recently Roy commented that the tiger was acting strange that night; it hadn't been acting like it-self.

Well, I'm no authority on tigers, but it seems to me the tiger was acting an awful lot like . . . well, like a tiger!

Some animal experts agree. "The cat wasn't trying to pro-tect him [Roy]," says Jonathan Kraft, who runs an organiza-tion called Keepers of the Wild. "The cat was going for the jugular. That was a typical killing bite. . . . I admire the guys, I just think they are sending a wrong message. The message needs to be: These are wild animals."[1]

Louis Dorfman, an animal behaviorist from Dallas, said Siegfried's account of an accidental mauling was "a beautiful story, but it just doesn't wash."[2] A tiger is a tiger. The old cliché is true: You can't tame a tiger.

This same principle rings true when it comes to God. Oh we might try to tame the Almighty. Dorothy Sayers observed that the church has "very efficiently pared the claws of the Lion of Judah, certified him 'meek and mild,' and recom-mended him as a fitting household pet for pale curates and pious old ladies."[3] You can try, but you cannot domesticate the Divine.

The Israelites tried—but with disastrous results. First Sam-uel tells the story:

> And Samuel's word came to all Israel.
>
> Now the Israelites went out to fight against the Philistines. The Israelites camped at Ebenezer, and the Philistines at Aphek. The Philistines deployed their forces to meet Israel, and as the battle spread, Israel was defeated by the Philistines, who killed about four thousand of them on the battlefield. When the soldiers returned to camp, the elders of Israel asked, "Why did the LORD bring defeat upon us today before the Philistines?

Let us bring the ark of the LORD's covenant from Shiloh, so that it may go with us and save us from the hand of our enemies" (1 Samuel 4:1–3).

The Israelites were at war against the Philistines. The Philistines had come to the Holy Land from across the sea—probably from Crete. They were known as the "Sea People." They believed in the real estate axiom "location, location, location," for they settled in the coveted coastal regions of Palestine along the Mediterranean Sea. They were regarded by the Israelites as cruel barbarians.

Now there is a reason why the Philistines were so feared by the Israelites. First Samuel 13:19 gives us a snapshot of the situation: "Not a blacksmith could be found in the whole land of Israel, because the Philistines had said, 'Otherwise the Hebrews will make swords or spears!' . . . So on the day of the battle not a soldier with Saul and Jonathan had a sword or spear in his hand." In the ancient world, new technology was emerging, but it was not accessible to all nations at the same time. The Philistines were living in the Iron Age. But "not a blacksmith could be found" in Israel. In other words, the Israelites were stuck in the Stone Age. To put it in contemporary nomenclature, the Philistines had weapons of mass destruction while Israel had slingshots.

So Israel went to war, and four thousand of their soldiers were massacred. The Israelites responded as you would expect. They debriefed each other, asking the obvious question: "What happened? Where was God? Why did the Lord bring defeat upon us today before the Philistines?"

Then one of the elders had an idea. He said, "I know! Let's go into battle again, only this time, we'll use our secret weapon. This time, let's bring the ark of the covenant with us."

The ark of the covenant was a gold-overlaid chest of acacia wood with two golden cherubim on the lid. The tablets of the law, or covenant, were housed inside this chest, and the ark itself resided first in the tabernacle Moses built, and later in the Most Holy Place of Solomon's temple in Jerusalem. It represented the presence of God within Israel. Where the ark was, God was. So the Israelites figured, "The Philistines have weapons crafted of iron; we've got the ark."

You see, bringing the ark into the battle was their way of cornering God. They were saying, "OK, Yahweh, *Your* reputation is on the line now. You *have* to come through in order to protect Your name. So long as we have God in a box and bring Him into our battle, we can't lose."

This represents a shift in thinking about God. No longer is He the supreme Being of the universe that all must humbly submit to. Rather, God becomes someone they can use. They figured, "We have God in a box."

Perhaps an episode of *The Simpsons* will help to illustrate. I am told there was a show where Homer pledged money to a PBS telethon. He never intended to pay the pledge; but he was tired of the commercials so he promised money he didn't have. Well the TV executives tracked Homer down. As punishment, he was forced to serve as a missionary on a Pacific island. (I realize it's a far-fetched plot, but hey, we're talking cartoons.) So during this mission, Homer's group built a new church. Now, Homer is not a spiritual guy; nevertheless, he was quite proud of their accomplishment. He stood at a distance admiring his work when he quipped, "Well, I don't know much about God, but we sure have built Him a nice little cage."

That's the way the Israelites had God figured. They were basically saying, "If things don't go our way, we've got the ark. We've got God in a box. We don't know much about God, but we sure built Him a nice little cage."

Now before we cast our aspersions at God's people of old, do you suppose we might be building cages for God as well?

John Ortberg, from whom I borrowed the Simpsons story, and some of the Bible commentary for this story, explains, "Sometimes, we think, 'If I just keep up my end of the spiritual bargain. . . . if I avoid scandals and a big sexual sin and keep my nose clean, or if I serve the church or I read the Bible, I tow the line, then God better keep up his end of the bargain.' "[4]

Recently a visitor at my church came to my office and shared her story of disillusionment with God. Seems her nineteen-year-old daughter had been diagnosed with a rare form of cancer and was given less than a month to live.

"I have served God for forty-two years," this woman said. "I have been active in my local church. I put my kids through Christian schools. I have obeyed the Ten Commandments. But now I'm giving up on God. I cannot love any God who would kill my girl."

I shared with her this story from 1 Samuel chapter 4 as a way to say that we cannot control God with our good deeds. Faithfulness is no guarantee that God will protect us from all harm. Being faithful doesn't obligate God to reward us accordingly.

Sure, I've been guilty of this same aberrant thinking. After graduating from the seminary, I entered the conference president's office with fear and trembling. He reported, "The conference executive committee has voted to put you at the North Creek Church."

"North Creek?" I questioned. "I didn't know there was a church at North Creek."

"Well, there's not. We want you to plant a church there."

I begged him to send me somewhere else—any other place would have been fine with me. I followed up with nasty phone calls and threatening letters. Finally he got back to me and said, "Karl, I feel so honored that you would feel safe enough with me to share your true feelings. Thank you for being so vulnerable. . . . Now go plant a church at North Creek."

That first Sabbath I preached to a congregation that consisted of my wife and one other couple. In the middle of my sermon the couple excused themselves, saying, "We promised some friends that we would meet them in the mountains. Sorry, we have to go." That left me preaching to my wife—which is never a good idea.

It was a hard run. At one point I was so discouraged I couldn't bring myself to write a sermon, to give a Bible study, or to lead those struggling saints any longer. I recall sitting at my desk in the corner of our unfinished basement scanning the classified ads in hopes of finding another job. But I wasn't qualified to do anything else.

My prayer was laced with anger. "God," I said, "this is not what I signed up for when I went into ministry. I could have made a mark in the business world or finished my studies for medicine, but no, I followed Your calling and went into the ministry. Now where are You? Is this dysfunctional, ragtag group of pitiful, petulant sheep all I get?"

In the middle of my prayer, the telephone rang. It was Keith, the head deacon at our church. He didn't even say "Hello." He just said, "Listen to me, Karl." At 6 feet, 3 inches, and 230 pounds, he had an intimidating presence—even on the phone. He growled, "I know we have been going through some turbulent times in the church, and I know it's not easy for you and Cherié. But if you ever think about quitting the ministry I will come over to your house and break both your legs. And remember: I know where you live." He hung up with no "Goodbye."

I returned to my prayer and mumbled, "God, You *could* be a little more subtle."

I'm ashamed to admit this, but I figured God was getting a pretty good deal with me. But God wasn't living up to my expectations. He wasn't blessing me with a big church or an influential pulpit or any book contracts.

When we try to put God in a box, we can get spiritually cocky and think we know all about Him. We always know the answer to the wristband WWJD. We know what radio station God listens to, the kind of worship He prefers, even the style of clothing He'd wear.

Soon we can develop a judgmental attitude toward others who don't see God as we *know* Him to be. And we can be theologically correct right down to our decaffeinated, nonalcoholic, smoke-free, vegan little souls—because we've got God in a box.

Brennan Manning writes,

> Clearly, the God of our imagination is not worthy of trust, adoration, praise, reverence, or gratitude. And yet, if we are unwilling to address the issue of transcendence, that is the only deity we know.

> The loss of transcendence has left in its wake the flotsam of distrustful, cynical Christians, angry at a capricious God, and the jetsam of smug bibliolatrists who claim to know precisely what God is thinking and exactly what he plans to do.[5]

But, what if it turns out that our God is not so tame? What if He is too feral and free to be controlled by our clever prayers and slick worship services and good behavior? What if our God is transcendent beyond our control?

The Israelites learned of the transcendence of God. "Where is God?" they asked. After all, they had just been decimated in a bloody battle with the Philistines. So they schemed to get the ark of the covenant and pick a fight with the Philistines again. Only this time they had God in a box. God would have to fight for them if they carried the ark, wouldn't He? Just as Siegfried and Roy thought they had tamed the wild tiger for their show, the Israelites thought they had God completely domesticated, but—again, like Siegfried and Roy—they were sadly mistaken.

So the people sent men to Shiloh, and they brought back the ark of the covenant of the LORD Almighty, who is enthroned between the cherubim. And Eli's two sons, Hophni and Phinehas, were there with the ark of the covenant of God.

When the ark of the LORD's covenant came into the camp, all Israel raised such a great shout that the ground shook. Hearing the uproar, the Philistines asked, "What's all this shouting in the Hebrew camp?"

When they learned that the ark of the LORD had come into the camp, the Philistines were afraid. "A god has come into the camp," they said. "We're in trouble! Nothing like this has happened before. Woe to us! Who will deliver us from the hand of these mighty gods? They are the gods who struck the Egyptians with all kinds of plagues in the desert. Be strong, Philistines! Be men, or you will be subject to the Hebrews, as they have been to you. Be men, and fight!"

So the Philistines fought, and the Israelites were defeated and every man fled to his tent. The slaughter was very great; Israel lost thirty thousand foot soldiers. The ark of God was captured, and Eli's two sons, Hophni and Phinehas, died (1 Samuel 4:4–11).

It was a very dark day for God's people. As it turned out, God would not be manipulated by some clever scheme to drag the ark into battle. God did not intervene on behalf of His nation.

The story that unfolds next in the Bible account describes a messenger who runs from the battlefield to Shiloh, eighteen miles away. He brings a message to Eli, the priest, who sits by the city gate anxiously waiting for the news. Eli is ninety-eight years old and blind.

If you notice closely, there is an interesting progression in the way the messenger delivers the news to Eli: It gets progressively worse. First, he reports, "Israel fled before the Philistines. We lost four thousand men."

Then he adds, "So, we retrieved the ark from Shiloh and returned to battle. This time we lost thirty thousand men." In the first battle they lost on the battlefield; in other words, at least they stood their ground. The second battle was so devastating that "every man fled to his tent" (verse 10).

Third piece of news: "Worse than that, Eli, your sons, Hophni and Phinehas, were both killed." Eli must face the harsh reality that he will have no one to care for him in his old age.

But the news gets even darker: "Uh, . . . um, . . . the unthinkable has happened," the messenger stammers. "The ark of the covenant has been captured."

In ancient literature, one of the ways a skillful storyteller emphasizes the most salient theme is by sheer repetition. It's a way of alerting the reader—without interrupting the flow of the story—"Here's what you need to pay attention to." In this case, the storyteller does just that. In verse 11, verse 13, verse 17, verse 19, verse 21, and in verse 22, the same message is repeated and repeated and repeated: "The ark of the covenant has been captured."

Why all the fuss about the ark of the covenant being captured? The answer comes from a most unlikely theologian—Eli's daughter-in-law, the wife of Phinehas. She is pregnant when she hears of her husband's death. She goes into premature labor. As she is giving birth, the midwife tries to encourage her by saying, "Don't despair. You've given birth to a son." In other words, even in the midst of all this death, there's still hope. But this anonymous widow will not be encouraged. "She named the boy Ichabod, saying, 'The glory has departed from Israel'—because of the capture of the ark of God" (verse 21).

The name *Ichabod* is the negative form of the word *kabod*. Figuratively, *kabod* means "glory." Where there was *kabod,* God was there. *Kabod* meant there was reason for hope.

In Hebrew, placing the letter *i* in front of a word makes it mean the opposite of its usual meaning. We have something similar in the English language with the letter *a*. For example, *amoral* is the opposite of *moral; asymmetrical* means "not symmetrical."

So Phinehas's wife names the child not *Kabod* ("glory") but *Ichabod,* ("no glory"). The glory has departed from Israel with the capture of the ark. "God has abandoned us." And then she dies of despair.

Don't miss the rich irony in this story. For as wild and fearsome as is this God of Israel, He still represents the safest place to live. Paradoxically, the greatest security comes in His presence. When the presence of God is gone, there's no reason to live.

There is something strangely comforting about living in the presence of this untamable God, as Rabbi Harold Kushner points out: "The next time you go to the zoo, notice where the lines are longest. . . . we find ourselves irresistibly drawn to the lions, the tigers, the elephants, the gorillas. Why? . . . [Because] we are strangely reassured at seeing creatures bigger and stronger than ourselves, creatures we did not make and who are not subject to our control. It gives us the message, at once humbling and comforting, that we are not the ultimate power. Our souls are so starved for that sense of awe, that encounter with grandeur which helps to remind us of our real place in the universe, that if we can't get it in church, we will search for it and find it someplace else."[6]

We desperately crave the reassuring reminder that human beings are not the last word. Thankfully, we do not possess ultimate power. We cannot tame God; we can only trust Him.

C. S. Lewis gave us a helpful picture of this untamable God. In his Narnia tales, Aslan represents Jesus. Mr. and Mrs. Beaver are explaining to the kids who Aslan is:

> I tell you he is the King of the wood and the son of the great Emperor-Beyond-the-Sea. Don't you know who is the King of the Beasts? Aslan is a lion—*the* Lion, the great Lion."
>
> "Ooh!" said Susan, "I thought he was a man. Is he—quite safe? I shall feel rather nervous about meeting a lion."
>
> "That you will, dearie, and no mistake," said Mrs. Beaver, "if there's anyone who can appear before Aslan without their knees knocking, they're either braver than most or just silly."
>
> "Then he isn't safe?" said Lucy.
>
> "Safe?" said Mr. Beaver. "Don't you hear what Mrs. Beaver tells you? Who said anything about safe? 'Course he isn't safe. But he's good. He's the King, I tell you."[7]

Our God is not safe. But He is good.

Jim Butcher comments, "If you want a God whose only mission is your safety and comfort, it's time to drop Jesus. Jesus calls us to great sacrifices and great challenges. And we follow, not because He's safe, but because He's King."[8]

Remember that the next time you feel like your name is Ichabod and you wonder, *Where is God?*

What should you do when your name is Ichabod? Well, in this story, there is no easy answer. There's no chapter titled,

"Six Simple Things You Can Do When You Feel Abandoned by God." Remember, we don't have God in a box.

Our only option is to persevere and trust God. Don't despair, don't give up, and don't cave in to your doubts. For if you keep holding on to Jesus, your story may unfold as it did for the Israelites. In the ancient tale we see an astonishing twist. What God does next will blow your mind.

God allows Himself to be taken captive! God permits the Philistines to drag His ark—the manifestation of His presence—through the streets of Ashdod. The Philistines have a grand parade as they mock and spit upon the God of Israel. Yahweh, unlike any other god, takes upon Himself the punishment of His people. What kind of God would do such a thing?

Ortberg points out that this is a foreshadowing of a day when God would be present on the earth, not in a box, not in an ark, but in a person.[9] The apostle John says, "And we beheld his *kabod* . . . and the word became flesh and dwelt among us" (see John 1:1–14). We beheld His glory, and it didn't look anything like what we imagined. This God didn't fit into the religious leaders' box of preconceived notions of the divine. He came to a stinky stable; He came with no authority or fame or wealth. And at the end of a tame life, he becomes a prisoner; His body, which was the manifestation of God on this earth—a kind of new ark of the covenant—is taken captive. It is spat upon on the road to Golgotha.

Then, on the cross God becomes Ichabod. He cries out, "God, where are You? Why have You forsaken Me? Why is My name Ichabod?" Then He gives up His life. His body—the manifestation of God on earth—is placed in a box. And Pontius Pilate posts a guard to stand watch to make sure nothing happens to this body; to make sure that the movement Jesus started is totally tamed, thoroughly domesticated.

Pilate figures, "I don't know much about this Jesus, but I sure have built him a nice little cage." But God won't be put in a cage. A tiger like Montecore may appear to be tame, but he's still a tiger. And a God like ours may seem, at times, to be meek and mild. But that's not all He is. He's still God.

On the third day Jesus exploded out of the box they tried to put Him in. And because He did, we can now flourish in the hope and the power and the presence of this magnificent and thoroughly untamable God.

Siegfried and Roy and Our Untamable God
(Questions for Reflection or Group Study)

1. What was your reaction when you heard the news about a tiger attacking Roy during a live show? Do you tend to sympathize more with Roy or the tiger? Explain your reasons.

2. Share your personal reaction to this quote by Dorothy Sayers: "[The church has] very efficiently pared the claws of the Lion of Judah, certified him 'meek and mild' and recommended him as a fitting household pet for pale curates and pious old ladies."

3. Describe a time when you were overwhelmed by the grand transcendence of God.

4. Have you ever tried to put God in a box? What happened?

5. How does the story of Ichabod help to address the question of where God is in our suffering?

6. Is there an area in your life where God is pressing you to persevere? How might you grow through the trial?

7. Do you tend to prefer a God who is meek and mild, or dangerous and unsafe? Why?

1. Adam Goldman, "Animal Experts Question Siegfried's Version of Tiger Attack," SignOnSanDiego.com, October 9, 2003, <-http://www.signonsandiego.com/news/nation/20031009-1433-nv-tigerattack-magician.html>.

2. NBC5.com, "Experts Say Tiger Attack on Illusionist Was Predatory," <http://www.nbc5.com/news/2549729/detail.html?z=dp&dpswid=2265994&dppid=65192/index.html>.

3. Dorothy Sayers, "The Greatest Drama," from *Spiritual Writings,* selected by Ann Loades (Boston: Cowley Publications, 1993), quoted at <http://www.bruderhof.com/articles/GreatestDrama.htm?format=print>.

4. John Ortberg, "Trusting When God Seems Absent, Part One," preached June 4, 2003, at Willow Creek Community Church, South Barrington, Illinois.

5. Brennan Manning, *Ruthless Trust* (San Francisco: HarperCollins Publishers, 2000), p. 81.

6. Harold Kushner, *Who Needs God* (New York: Summit Books, 1989), pp. 57, 58.

7. C. S. Lewis, *The Lion, the Witch and the Wardrobe* (New York: Collier, 1970), pp. 75, 76.

8. Jim Butcher, "Is Jesus Safe," <http://www.mywv.net/cities/poca/pocabaptist/articles/isjesussafe.htm>.

9. John Ortberg, "Trusting When God Seems Absent, Part One," preached June 4, 2003, at Willow Creek Community Church, South Barrington, Illinois.

Chapter five

Seeing Your Way
Through Suffering

Stephen Hawking, the astrophysicist at Cambridge University, has been labeled the most intelligent human being on earth. He has advanced the general theory of relativity beyond the bounds of anyone since Albert Einstein. Stephen Hawking, however, is afflicted with ALS syndrome (Lou Gehrig's disease). Eventually, the disease will claim his life. Until then, he suffers greatly under the curse. He has been confined to a wheelchair for years, where he can do little more than sit and think. Hawking cannot speak. He can communicate only by means of a computer that is operated from the tiniest movement of his fingertips.

According to *Omni* magazine, "He is too weak to write, feed himself, comb his hair, fix his glasses—all this must be done for him. Yet this most dependent of all men has escaped invalid status. His personality shines through the messy details of his existence."[1]

Before Hawking became ill, he had minimal interest or motivation in life. He called it a "pointless existence" resulting from sheer boredom. He was a borderline alcoholic and did very little work. Then he discovered he had Lou Gehrig's disease. The doctors informed him he would probably die within two years. The ultimate effect of that diagnosis, beyond its initial shock, was extremely positive. He claimed to have been happier after he was afflicted than before. How could that be? Listen to Hawking's answer: "When one's expectations are reduced to zero, one really appreciates everything that one does have."[2]

Stated another way, contentment in life is determined in

part by what a person anticipates from it. To a man like Hawking (who thought he would soon die), everything takes on meaning—a sunrise, a walk in a park, the laughter of children. By sailing through a hurricane, Hawking discovered a richness and texture of life that would not be possible on placid waters.

Malcolm Muggeridge put it this way: "I can say with complete truthfulness that everything I have learned in my seventy-five years in this world, everything that has truly enhanced and enlightened my experience, has been through affliction and not through happiness."[3]

Tim Hansel points out that some of the greatest human accomplishments were born out of suffering. For example, most of the Psalms emerged from heartache. Most of the epistles were penned in prisons. Florence Nightingale reorganized the hospitals of England from a bed, too sick to move. Francis Parkman, the American historian, was in so much pain that he could not work longer than five minutes at a time. His eyesight was so weak that he was forced to write gigantic words in order to see what he had written. Nevertheless, he authored twenty classic volumes of history.

"Sometimes it seems that when God is about to make pre-eminent use of a man, he puts him through the fire."[4]

Ellen White offers this perspective: "Those who are willing to suffer for Christ will experience more joy in suffering than in the fact that Christ has suffered for them, thus showing that He loved them. Those who win heaven will put forth their noblest efforts, and will labor with all long-suffering, that they may reap the fruit of toil."[5]

BRISTLECONE CHRISTIANS

Speaking to early Christian believers, the apostle Peter wrote that trials came to them "so that your faith—of greater worth than gold, which perishes even though refined by fire—

may be proved genuine and may result in praise, glory and honor when Jesus Christ is revealed" (1 Peter 1:7). The Bible teaches that our faith is refined by the fires we endure.

A symbol of this spiritual principle is the bristlecone pine. It's an unusual tree that grows in the mountain regions of western America, sometimes as high as two miles above sea level. These evergreens often live for thousands of years. Amazingly, the older specimens often have only one thin layer of bark.

Considering the habitat of these trees—rocky areas where the soil is poor and precipitation is rare—it seems inconceivable that they should live so long or even survive at all. The adversities of their environment, however, actually contribute to their longevity. These perverse conditions produce cells that are densely arranged, and many resin canals form within the plant. Wood that is so structured lives for a long, long time. In contrast, bristlecone pines growing in milder conditions grow faster, but soon decay and die. The harshness of their surroundings is a vital factor in making the trees strong and sturdy.

Similarly, Peter tells us that our faith is refined by fire. In other words, the harshness of our surroundings is a vital factor in making us strong and sturdy people of faith.

Christians mature into the likeness of Christ through adversity and suffering. Scripture teaches, "No discipline seems pleasant at the time, but painful. Later on, however, it produces a harvest of righteousness and peace for those who have been trained by it" (Hebrews 12:11).

Perhaps you're in a season of suffering. Your husband's drinking is escalating out of control. Your colleague at work slandered you. Your girlfriend rejected you. Your pet died. The tumor is malignant.

Instead of complaining, claim God's promise that "after you have suffered a little while, [God] will Himself restore you and make you strong, firm and steadfast" (1 Peter 5:10). Persevere!

God gave the children of Israel an annual feast celebrating the value of perseverance—the Feast of Sukkot. This feast commemorates the forty years the Jews wandered in the wilderness. Although it was only two hundred miles from Egypt to Canaan, it took God's people forty years to make the trip— a trek that should have taken no longer than a couple weeks!

The Feast of Sukkot reminds us of the value of suffering in the desert. It was during this time that the Israelites received the Ten Commandments and the pattern for the tabernacle. In the wilderness, a new generation emerged ready to enter the Promised Land.

The most significant kinds of growth cannot be hurried. A nation of slaves needs longer than two weeks to be transformed into a nation of free people. A man needs longer than a few years to develop a deep abiding trust in God. A woman needs time to paint a masterpiece. Great accomplishments grow out of wilderness experiences.

So when suffering sabotages your soul, take heart. God is growing you into the kind of person only He knows you can become. Instead of collapsing in despair, remind yourself of Madeleine L'Engle's words:

"We do not have to understand God's ways, or the suffering and brokenness and pain that sooner or later come to us all.

But we do have to know in the very depths of our being that the ultimate end of the story, no matter how many aeons it takes, is going to be all right."[6]

Seeing Your Way Through Suffering
(Questions for Reflection or Group Study)

1. What is the hardest thing you've had to endure?
2. What did God teach you in your trial?

3. Based on your experience, how does suffering affect your soul?

4. If you were given a month to live, how would you live the remainder of your life? What prevents you from living that way today?

5. What factors have been most formative in your spiritual life? What role has suffering played in your spiritual formation?

6. Hebrews 12:11 promises a "harvest of righteousness and peace" for those who endure pain. Is pain the only way to enjoy this harvest? Explain your answer.

7. What would you call your Feast of Sukkot? Describe a desert experience that now you would celebrate.

8. Can you think of someone going through a difficult time? Contact that person and offer your support.

9. Reflect on this statement by Madeleine L'Engle: "We do not have to understand God's ways, or the suffering and brokenness and pain that sooner or later come to us all. But we do have to know in the very depths of our being that the ultimate end of the story, no matter how many aeons it takes, is going to be all right."

1. Quoted in <http://www.sermonillustrations.com/a-z/s/suffering.htm>.

2. Ibid.

3. Ibid.

4. Tim Hansel, *You Gotta Keep Dancin'* (Elgin, Ill.: David C. Cook Publishing Company, 1985), p. 87.

5. Ellen White, *Selected Messages,* book 2, p. 166. Notebook Leaflets from the Elmshaven Library, 1985, "An Ernest Appeal," NBL, p. 74.

6. Madeleine L'Engle, "Glimpses of Grace," *Christianity Today,* vol. 42, no. 2, as quoted in *Bible Illustrator,* Index 372–374.

—Chapter six—
The Red Sox
Pitch for Hope

Shortly after the Red Sox won the World Series in 2004, I received this telephone message: "Pastor Haffner, this is Margaret. You don't know my husband and me because we're lost in the congregation, but we enjoyed your sermon a couple years ago about having faith in the Boston Red Sox. Ever since that sermon we've been quietly rooting for them as the little train that could. So, are you going to mention anything at church tomorrow in your sermon about how faith can be rewarded? About the Red Sox winning, that kind of ragtag team? I hope so, because it is an element of faith that has been rewarded."

For the record I did *not* gloat about my Red Sox from the pulpit the next day in church. I wanted to be humble about it. I wanted to be sensitive to New York Yankees fans after the Red Sox came back from a 3-0 deficit to win their best-of-seven series. I wanted to wait . . . until I had a reading audience of thousands and thus preserve in print forever the great news of Beantown's good fortune.

Growing up in Providence, Rhode Island, I have always been a die-hard Red Sox fan. And year after year after year I had my hopes dashed. Do you have any idea how much therapy it requires to process Mookie Wilson's ground ball that dribbled through the legs of Bill Buckner when the Red Sox could have won the series in 1986? That one play seemed to define the Boston Red Sox. Year after year the Yankees were in contention while my boys were home come October.

For the record, it does not take any courage to cheer for the Yankees. You know how many times the Yankees have won the series since 1918—the year the Red Sox last won a World Series? Twenty-six times! That's why Jesus said, "If ye root for the Yankees, I tell you the truth, you have your reward in full. But if ye root for the Red Sox, thou wilt develop a character for the kingdom. Thou shalt become a person of HOPE!"

I even published an article in *Insight* magazine about the spiritual implications of the Red Sox woes. This is how I concluded that article:

> Red Sox fans learn to hope. But really, we're all hopers. Hope is what prompts us to get back on the field and try again. Hope is the heartbeat of life.
>
> Conversely, doubt destroys us. "Doubt," says James Allen, "has killed more splendid projects, shattered more ambitious schemes, strangled more effective geniuses, neutralized more superb efforts, blasted more fine intellects, thwarted more splendid ambitions than any other enemy of the human race."[1]
>
> So dare to dream. Squash the doubts that whisper:
>
> "I'll never get into medical school."
>
> "This world is nothing but evil."
>
> "Jesus couldn't love somebody like me."
>
> When you feed such doubts, you suffocate the soul. But hope breathes life and energy into every crevice of your character.
>
> So hang on to hope. Even in a world racked with war and pain we can chill in the assurance that someday soon we'll be with our Father, safe at home.[2]

Shortly after that article was published, I got a card from

a woman in Yonkers, New York. She wrote:

> Dear Brother K:
>
> I just wanted to tell you how much I appreciated your lesson study in the October 11, 2003 issue of *Insight*. I was going through a serious bout of depression. Absolutely nothing was going right in my life. I was angry and sad. God didn't seem to hear my cries for help. Then I picked up the magazine and read it. *Your words made me cry with relief!* I was on the subway this morning, and a street preacher had shouted the same concern about how we as Christians should be more like the Red Sox fans. God is working through you. I wanted you to know that. My faith and hope have been restored! God *will* help me, He promised, and *I love Him for that.*
>
> With deep felt gratitude, a sister in Christ.

When the Red Sox were trailing three games to none against the Yankees in the American League Championship series I found this woman's letter and read it again. I reminded myself that there was no reason to relinquish hope. And sure enough, the Red Sox pulled off the most dramatic comeback in the history of professional sports.

What fueled the comeback? In a word, it was "hope."

Now I have to confess that nowhere does the Bible really say that the Red Sox are favored by God, but the Bible is bursting with passages about hope.

Listen to the apostle Paul: "I consider that our present sufferings are not worth comparing with the glory that will be revealed in us. The creation waits in eager expectation for the sons of God to be revealed. For the creation was subjected to frustration" (Romans 8:18–20).

Notice that, ironically, in order to have hope you must first have frustrations. Hope is born out of problems. If you have everything you want and never encounter problems, you will never have the opportunity to learn how to keep hoping in spite of problems. You will never grow.

Back to the text:

> For the creation was subjected to frustration, not by its own choice, but by the will of the one who subjected it, in hope that the creation itself will be liberated from its bondage to decay and brought into the glorious freedom of the children of God.
>
> We know that the whole creation has been groaning as in the pains of childbirth right up to the present time (verses 20–22).

Paul uses a striking metaphor here. He compares the groaning of all creation to the cries of a woman in childbirth.

How much pain is there in childbirth? My wife assures me that I will never know and that I have no business writing about it. Others claim that the closest a male can come to experiencing the pain of childbirth is by passing a kidney stone. My brother showed me one that he passed. After all his groaning I fully expected to see something eight pounds, six ounces. But no, his pain trophy was smaller than a pea! I suspect my wife is right that guys don't get it on this one; so we had better move on to the next verse.

"Not only so, but we ourselves, who have the firstfruits of the Spirit, groan inwardly as we wait eagerly for our adoption as sons, the redemption of our bodies" (verse 23). Notice that Paul includes himself and his brothers and sisters in Rome among the groaners. Sometimes people think that becoming a Christian ought to mean that we're exempt from disappointment—that our prayers should all get answered just the way we want. As a Christian, my life ought to be pain free, right?

Paul doesn't promise that. We all know that Christians have car wrecks. We get fired. We get cancer. Crabgrass grows in our lawns too. What the Bible teaches is that Christians groan like everyone else in this sin-saturated world, but we groan with a sense of hope.

Consider the experience of Lewis Smedes. He tells of the hope of having a baby that he and his wife, Doris, shared. For ten years they pleaded with God for the desire of their hearts. At last God answered their prayer, and Doris was pregnant. But the baby threatened to come three months early. That's when the doctor told them the child would be seriously malformed. Lewis Smedes remembers:

> We decided that we were not going to give up hope. No matter what the doctor said, we were not going to give up hope. So we kept on hoping all through the night.
>
> At six o'clock in the morning, the doctor came to me with a somewhat embarrassed grin from ear to ear. He said, "Congratulations! You have a perfect baby boy. Come and see." I went with him, and there he was, yelling his head off, looking just like me—a perfect manchild. Praise God! We thought.
>
> It's true. Never give up hope. Never, ever give up hope.
>
> But two days later our baby was dead. Hope can break your heart.[3]

Yes, the groaning still comes. But hope anyway. For "it is not the way we deal with our human situation that is the basis for hope—hope is the basis for how we deal with our human situation."[4]

Paul then reminds us, "For in this hope we were saved" (verse 24). In Paul's day, this belief that we are saved in hope was unique to the Christian faith. Dallas Willard points out, "One of the remarkable changes brought on by Jesus and His people into the ancient world concerned the elevation of hope into a primary virtue. Hope was not well regarded by the Greco-Roman world."[5]

The Greeks taught that you're better off to not get your hopes up. They believed hoping was a sure set-up for disappointment.

Jesus introduced a radical new concept of hope. Paul built on the teaching of Christ when he said that Christians can face the future with great confidence because our hope does not depend on us; rather, it is our hope in Christ by which we are saved. Jesus sent His Spirit so you and I could become hopers.

"But hope that is seen is no hope at all. Who hopes for what he already has? But if we hope for what we do not yet have, we wait for it patiently" Paul continues (verses 24, 25).

Dr. Jerome Groopman is a professor at Harvard Medical School, a practicing physician, a leading researcher in the fight against cancer and AIDS, and an author. He discovered that all of his patients were looking for a sense of genuine hope—and indeed, that hope was as important to them as anything he might prescribe as a physician.

After writing a book called *The Anatomy of Hope*, Groopman was asked for his definition of hope. He said, "Basically, I think hope is the ability to see a path to the future. . . . You are facing dire circumstances, and you need to know everything that's blocking or threatening you. And then you see a path, or a potential path, to get to where you want to be. Once you see that, there's a tremendous emotional uplift that occurs, and with it actual neurochemical and biological changes."[6]

He continued, "I think hope has been, is, and always will be the heart of medicine and healing. . . . [Even with all the medical technology available to us now], we still come back to this profound human need to believe that there is a possibility to reach a future that is better than the one in the present."[7]

The Word of God teaches us that there is indeed a path to a brighter future. It is Jesus Christ, who said, "I am the way" (John 14:6). "In this hope," the apostle Paul tells us, "we were saved" (Romans 8:24).

So keep on hoping. When the Yankees are up three to zip, hope. When you're facing cutbacks at work, hope. When your kids have left the church, hope.

In the end, the soul is fueled by this one thing—hope.

The Red Sox Pitch for Hope
(Questions for Reflection or Group Study)

1. What's your favorite baseball team? Why?
2. What are you hoping for?
3. Who's the most hope-filled person you know? What makes this person so hopeful?
4. Read Romans 8:18–25. Explain the connection between creation and hope.
5. Discuss the difference between hope and wishful thinking.
6. How would you define hope?
7. In your life right now, where is God asking you to hang on to hope?

1. James Allen, <http://www.phnet.fi/public/mamaa1/quotesnf. htm>.

2. Karl Haffner, "Doubt," *Insight*, October 11, 2003, pp. 14, 15.

3. Lewis Smedes, "Keep Hope Alive," Preaching Today, tape no. 139.

4. Arden K. Barden, "Spiritual Aging," *Christianity Today,* vol. 32, no. 1.

5. John Ortberg in "The Power of Hope," at <http://www.mppc.org/ e_sermons/esermon_2003/apr_03/4_27_03.html>, p. 4.

6. Jerome Groopman, quoted by Rachel K. Sobel, "The Mysteries of Hope and Healing," USNews.com, <http://www.usnews.com/usnews/ health/articles/040126/26conv.htm>.

7. Ibid.

Soul Community

"The soul hardly ever realizes it,

but whether he is a believer or not,

his loneliness

is really a homesickness for God."

(Hubert van Zeller, 1905–1984)

Chapter seven

Created for Community

I couldn't figure it out. When I read the letter that was addressed to the president of Pontiac Division of General Motors, I assumed it was from some nitwit who was a few screws short of a healthy carburetor. As it turns out, however, the author wasn't wacky at all. Perhaps you can solve the dilemma. Here's the letter:

> This is the second time I've written to you, and I don't blame you for not answering me, because what I have to say sounds kind of crazy. But it is a fact that we have a tradition in our family of ice cream for dessert after dinner each night. But the kind of ice cream varies. So every night, after we've eaten, the whole family votes on which kind of ice cream we should have, and I drive down to the store to get it. I want you to know I'm serious about this question, no matter how silly it sounds. What is there about a Pontiac that makes it not start when I get vanilla ice cream and easy to start whenever I get any other kind?

The president at Pontiac was skeptical but, nonetheless, sent an engineer to investigate. When the engineer arrived, he was surprised to meet a family who seemed extraordinarily normal! They were celebrating vanilla night, and he joined them for a trip to the ice cream store. Much to the engineer's surprise, after the family purchased the vanilla ice cream, the car would not start!

The following night, the engineer joined the family for chocolate ice cream night. As predicted, the car fired right up with no problem. The next night it was strawberry ice cream. Again, no problem with the Pontiac. The following night was vanilla night again. Sure enough, the car refused to start.

Any idea why? If you're stumped, don't sweat it—the engineer couldn't readily solve the mystery either. He collected voluminous notes tracking every variable from the brand of gas being used to the weather on each night. Finally, he figured it out.

The answer was in the amount of time spent in the store. Vanilla, being the most popular flavor of ice cream, was in a freezer by itself in the front of the store. The store manager had thoughtfully provided this convenience to save time for his customers. As a result, it took less time for the Pontiac owner to buy vanilla than any other flavor.

Because the owner spent less time in the store getting vanilla ice cream, the car had less time to cool down, and a vapor lock formed. The reason the car wouldn't start wasn't vanilla ice cream; it was vapor lock.

When my friend Pastor Greg Nelson shared this story with me, I wondered if it was not a parable of life. How often do we fail to solve our real problems because we don't dig to the heart of the matter? We seem obsessed with ice cream solutions for vapor lock dilemmas. We run to the bedroom to mask our loneliness. We race to the movies to address our boredom. We hurry to the refrigerator to quiet our soul hunger. And after all that, we still grapple with empty souls and troubled spirits—because the answer we desperately seek will be found only in God.

Until we are intimately connected to God and to His community we will feel lonely, isolated, and discontented. Only in fellowship with God and His followers will our souls find quiet. Erich Fromm had it right when he said, "The deepest need of man is the need to overcome his separateness, to leave the prison of his aloneness."[1]

To address human aloneness God established community. So deeply is this value of community embedded in the character of God that we find it before Creation, during Creation, and after Creation.

BEFORE CREATION

First, consider what was before Creation. There was God. Listen to how the prophet Isaiah described God. God says, "Here is my servant, [speaking of His Son, Jesus Christ] whom I uphold, my chosen one in whom I delight; I will put my Spirit [speaking of the Holy Spirit] on him and he will bring justice to the nations" (Isaiah 42:1).

This is one of numerous references in Scripture that distinguish between the roles of the three persons of the Trinity. Isaiah 48:16 puts it like this: "And now the Sovereign LORD [this is God, the Father] has sent me, [Jesus Christ, the One sent by God] with his Spirit [a reference to the Holy Spirit]."

Before Creation, God existed in community. Moreover, God invites us into this fellowship of the Trinity.

Jesus prayed, "My prayer is not for them alone. I pray also for those who will believe in me through their message, that all of them may be one, Father, just as you are in me and I am in you. May they also be in us so that the world may believe that you have sent me" (John 17:20, 21). Jesus prayed for His followers to be "in us." In other words, He invites us into the fellowship of the Trinity.

In the movie *Meet the Parents*, a young man, played by Ben Stiller, can't seem to win over his future father-in-law, a retired CIA officer. Throughout the movie the dad mentions his "circle of trust"—referring to those few but deserving individuals who are accepted into his private world. But the kid can't crack into the circle.

Scripture teaches that God invites you and me into His circle of trust. In reflecting on this profound truth, a family vacation comes to mind. I was only nine years old, and yet I remember it well. We were in Washington D.C., strolling down Pennsylvania Avenue when a guard at the White House stopped my dad and grilled him with questions.

"Is this your family?"

"Yes," Dad answered.

"Where are you from?"

"Providence, Rhode Island."

"What are you doing here?"

"We're just on vacation."

The security officer smiled. "Today's your lucky day."

He motioned for us to follow him, leading us to a private gathering at the Rose Garden. There were only a few people there (mostly reporters) to welcome a dignitary from China. Joining our small party was the thirty-seventh president of the United States of America, Richard Nixon. Here we were, hobnobbing with the most powerful person on the planet, as if we were part of his inner circle.

That would never happen today. At least, it couldn't happen with the earthly powers that be. And yet Jesus prayed that it would happen for us with the heavenly powers. We are invited into His circle of intimacy. God longs for us to enjoy intimate community with Him.

AT CREATION

Not only do we see community at the core of who God is *before* Creation, but community is clear *at* Creation as well.

"Then God said, 'Let us make man in our image, in our likeness, and let them rule over the fish of the sea and the birds of the air, over the livestock, over all the earth, and over all the creatures that move along the ground' " (Genesis 1:26).

Notice that God refers to Himself in the plural form—"let *us* make man in *our* image, in *our* likeness." Why the plural form? Because God is Three in One; by nature, He is plural.

There is a refrain that keeps recurring in the story of Creation: "And God said, 'Let there be light,' and there was light. God saw that the light was good" (Genesis 1:3, 4).

Day after day during Creation week, we find this refrain: "And God said . . . and it was so . . . and God saw that it was good." It's the song of Creation.

It's not until the final act of Creation that this song screeches to a halt. God creates man, and He proclaims, "It is not good for the man to be alone" (Genesis 2:18). Clearly, God is making a statement about the fundamental importance of human relationships. We were created in the image of God—who is community—for community. God Himself declared that it is not good to do life in isolation.

What a timely and relevant reminder this is in an era that has witnessed a great erosion of community. Robert Putnam, in his book *Bowling Alone,* suggests that for twenty-five years American society has experienced a steady decline of "social capital"—a sense of connectedness and community. This bankruptcy in social capital has wreaked devastating results: more depression, poorer educational performance, an increase in teen pregnancies—to mention just a few of the negative side effects.

The era of the Waltons is over. Neighbors helping neighbors, unhurried conversations on the porch swing, families eating meals together—these vignettes hearken back to simpler times when life revolved around relationships. But that's not today.

There's a story flying around the Internet that takes us back to those good old days. Seems a farm boy named Willis overturned a wagonload of wheat. Willis wasn't concerned because he knew some neighbor would give him a hand. You see, in those days neighbors looked out for one another.

Sure enough, a nearby farmer showed up to help. "Hey, Willis," he said, "forget your troubles for a while and come and have dinner with us. Then I'll help you set the wagon back upright."

"That's very nice of you," Willis answered, "but I don't think Dad would like me to do that."

"Aw, come on, son!" the farmer insisted.

"Well, OK," the boy finally agreed, "but Dad won't like it."

After a hearty dinner, Willis thanked the host. "I feel a lot better now, but I know Dad's going to be real upset."

"Don't be silly!" said the neighbor. "By the way, where is your dad?"

Willis replied, "He's stuck under the wagon!"

OK, so maybe sitting around the neighbor's dinner table is not always a good thing! In most cases, however, I'll still take that over the frantic, frenzied, never-have-time-for-anybody pace we've got going today.

When you boil it down, what is more important? A better paying job? A higher grade? A bigger house? A faster boat? All of these things are good, but they're not as important as community.

AFTER CREATION

This deep human longing for community continues to this day. That's one reason God established His church. Ephesians 4:3 reminds us to "make every effort to keep the unity of the Spirit through the bond of peace." We are commanded in Scripture to do whatever it takes to preserve community. In this verse, Paul uses a rare Greek verb to suggest intense urgency. It could be translated, "Do it now! Pay any price! Spare no pain! Whatever it takes, do it!" The apostle pleads with a sense of urgency to keep unity in the church. He is saying, "Be intentional about nurturing a sense of community in the church. This is a life or death matter."

One of the most famous research projects that has ever been done on community is called the Alameda County Study. It was headed by a Harvard social scientist, and it took place over a nine-year period. Researchers tracked the lives of seven thousand people—residents of Alameda County in California. They found, among other things, that the most isolated people were three times more likely to die than the most relationally connected people.

Community is literally a matter of life or death. That was certainly the case for Neil Watts. He is the president of the Queensland Conference of Seventh-day Adventists. Recently I enjoyed a dinner with Neil; our conversation drifted to near-death experiences. (We were in Australia, and I spoke of tasting Marmite Yeast Spread as a near-death experience.)

Neil shared a story of when he was president of the Western Pacific Union Mission of Seventh-day Adventists back in 1999. Twelve people (the pilot, an airline engineer, Neil, and nine other passengers) boarded a commercial flight in Vanuatu. The flight started out smoothly until they hit a storm. Neil told me that he heard the engines quit and assumed they were about to crash into a mountain. Instead, they crashed into shark-infested waters five miles from shore.

Neil scrambled onto the wing, where he pulled off his shoes and pants so he could swim more freely. In less than two minutes the plane slipped nose-down into the water, taking with it the pilot and three of the passengers. The remaining eight persons were all alone in the dark and the cold.

Neil called out, "We're obviously in trouble here, but if any of you have faith in God, I'm a minister, and I'm going to pray. You can join me in prayer if you want."

You're probably not surprised to learn that in that moment he had some takers! Over the roar of the wind and the pounding of rain Neil shouted as loud as he could, asking God to care for them.

Six of the survivors determined to keep together. Only one in the group had a life jacket. Another member of the group drifted away. This was a fatal mistake; English newspapers would later report his death due to a shark attack.

The five remaining determined to stay together. At one point they saw a freighter, but no one on the ship saw them. Later they saw a fishing boat, but again that proved to be a false hope.

In an article in the *Adventist Review* Neil remembered the night this way:

> After about four hours, I was close to exhaustion. I figured I would probably die and wondered what it would be like. I thought that others in the group might also not make it and that they could die without knowing Christ. I'm sure the Lord prompted me, and I called out to the others, reminding them of some of the wonderful promises of Jesus that tell us that no matter what happens to us, if we believe and trust in Him we can have assurance of eternal life.
>
> My body was hurting terribly, and I felt like taking a deep breath, diving as deep as I could, opening my mouth, and letting it happen. I just hoped it wouldn't take long.

I thought of myself dead, and everything else going on without me. I worried about Joy and how she would manage. I hoped she would find someone who would look after her.[2]

Neil told me that he is not a strong swimmer. No one in that group claimed to be a good swimmer. I wondered, *So what was it that kept them going?* Neil shared that the thing that kept them going had to do with community. When one of the people in their small group would falter, the others rallied and insisted that every one hang on. They were determined to survive together.

After six hours they collapsed together on the shore. They called out to God in grateful thanks for sparing their lives.

I was mesmerized as Neil shared his story. He finished by saying, "My priorities have changed, and I have become more focused. When you come down to it, it's only your relationship to God and your family that really matter. You can lose everything else."

Boil it all down, and what matters is community—your relationship with God and others.

Created for Community
(Questions for Reflection or Group Study)

1. What's your favorite flavor of ice cream? Did you figure out the ice cream mystery before you read what the problem was? Have you ever had a time when you tried to solve a deeper problem by using a surface solution?

2. Who is your closest friend? What makes that friendship different from other friendships? Who is in your circle of trust?

3. Discuss the statement "Only in fellowship with God and His followers will our souls find quiet."

4. Have you found Robert Putnam's premise—that we are much more disconnected today than we used to be—to be true in your life? Why or why not?

5. In a small group, make a list titled "Twenty-One Ways to Nurture Community."

6. Have you ever had a near-death experience? If so, did the experience color the way you looked at your close relationships? In what ways?

7. Community: What does it look like? Sound like? Feel like?

---

1. Quoted in Frank W. Harrington, "Four Foundational Questions: #3—'Am I Traveling Alone?' " Quoted in Peachtree Presbyterian Pulpit <http://www.peachtreepresb.org/sermons/wfh100498.htm>.

2. Neil Watts as told to William G. Johnsson, "Alive," *Adventist Review,* online edition, <http://www.adventistreview.org/9949/story1. htm>.

—Chapter eight—
The Gospel of Getting Stoned

To love and to be loved—that's the fiercest hunger of the human heart. Every soul craves community.

A number of studies would bear this out. For example, in Bonn, Germany, a group of psychologists, physicians, and insurance companies collaborated to research the secret of longevity and success. They stumbled upon a surprising discovery—those men who had fewer accidents on their way to work, missed less work because of sickness, and earned roughly 25 percent more money all shared a common thread that wound through their stories. What was that common thread? What was the secret of this group's success?

A kiss. Yes, that's right, a good-old fashioned smooch turns out to be more than a soap opera staple. According to Germany's Dr. Arthur Szabo, a husband who kisses his wife each morning has a positive attitude and functions better than the husband who fails to kiss his wife each morning.[1] Why would this be? I suspect the kissers enjoy better intimacy and community than do the nonkissers.

So do you want to make more money? Have fewer accidents? Be more productive at work? Kiss your spouse every morning!

Now this raises a practical point. People sometimes ask me: "What if I'm not married?" Well I say, "Kiss somebody! Do it in the name of highway safety, work productivity, do it for love of your country, but kiss somebody!" The point is, stay connected. You'll live longer.

Jesus understood the importance of community. He prayed for it. He nurtured it in His small group. He modeled it in a number of compelling snapshots. Take for example this story recorded in the Gospel of John: "But Jesus went to the Mount of Olives. At dawn he appeared again in the temple courts, where all the people gathered around him, and he sat down to teach them. The teachers of the law and the Pharisees brought in a woman caught in adultery. They made her stand before the group and said to Jesus, 'Teacher, this woman was caught in the act of adultery. In the Law Moses commanded us to stone such women' " (John 8:1–5).

The church leaders were correct. The penalty for adultery was death by stoning. (Now I hasten to add that when the Bible talks about being "stoned," it's talking about having rocks thrown at you—not getting high on drugs or alcohol! I don't want you to think that Jesus or the Bible condones getting "stoned" in the way we often use the term!) Leviticus 20:10 commands, "If a man commits adultery with another man's wife—with the wife of his neighbor—both the adulterer and the adulteress must be put to death." In the case of adultery, according to the Mishnah, the Jewish codified law, "The man is to be enclosed in dung up to his knees, and a soft towel set within a rough towel is to be placed around his neck (in order that no mark may be made, for the punishment is God's punishment). Then one man draws in one direction and another in the other direction, until he be dead."[2] The Mishnah also stipulates that if a woman is caught in adultery she is to be stoned to death.

So the Pharisees cornered Jesus and asked Him, " 'Now what do you say?' They were using this question as a trap, in order to have a basis for accusing him" (John 8:5, 6).

Whatever Jesus says, the church leaders intended to have Him trapped. If He said to stone the woman, they could accuse Him to the Romans, for Roman law did not allow the Jews to sentence anyone to death without the approval of the Roman officials. If He said not to stone her, then He would clearly be going against the law of Moses. But you know what Jesus did: "Jesus bent down and started to write on the ground with his finger. When they kept on questioning him, he straightened up and said to them, 'If any one of you is without sin, let him be the first to throw a stone at her' " (John 8:6, 7).

I must tell you when I first learned of this text. I was a junior in high school at Shenandoah Valley Academy in New Market, Virginia. The night before home leave word leaked out in the dorm about a big bash up in Nestler's room. So after the lights went out, I sneaked up to room 321—only to discover that Nestler had transformed the place into a candlelit casino. The agenda for the night was a penny poker tournament. (I'm not condoning the activity, I'm just telling a story.)

Although I had never played poker before (that is, after all, the reason parents spend a zillion dollars to send their kids to a private boarding academy—to learn such life skills—right?), by 3:00 A.M. I was 476 pennies richer! I wondered, *Am I supposed to pay tithe on my windfall?*

By 3:00 A.M. we were getting hungry.

"I'm famished," Kevin sighed.

"I know! Let's raid the cafeteria," Tim suggested.

"Great idea!" came the chorus of agreement.

"But what if we get caught?" someone weakly protested.

"Nonsense!" Nestler barked. "Everybody is doing it. You can practically letter in the sport. C'mon, let's go earn a Twinkie to decorate our class jackets."

"Yea!" we roared, as if responding to a pep talk from the coach.

We slinked across campus. After crawling through an unlocked window in the cafeteria, we froze at the sound of an unusual noise.

"Zzzzzzzzzzz."

Peaking into the pantry, we discovered Mr. Strickland, the vice principal. He was fed up (pun intended) with thieves on campus. He was determined to catch the culprits. The only problem was that Mr. Strickland was not operating in his arena of spiritual giftedness. He proved to be much too sound a sleeper to pull off this sting.

So while he snored, we passed éclairs, Doritos, and Little Debbies over his nose. With the backpacks full, we blew Mr. Strickland a kiss goodnight and disappeared.

Recently I saw Mr. Strickland and asked for permission to tell this story. "Tell it all you want." He grinned. "You can even use my name." Then he added this postscript: "By the way, Karl, you know you would have never been caught had you boys just kept your mouths shut."

Of course. But a story this good you have to share. Right? And share we did.

Next thing we knew we were sitting outside the principal's office waiting a turn to face the disciplinary committee. Kevin, Tim, Nestler, Dave, and others each took a turn to go face the firing squad. The last student to go in was Jeff.

"Young man," the principal growled as he peered over smudged glasses, "is there anything else you wish to tell this committee before we punish the whole lot of you?"

It was in that moment that Jeff quoted John 8:7: "Let he who is without sin cast the first stone."

The boy's dean told me later that at that moment he fell off his chair—he was laughing so hard. To this day I'm convinced this verse saved me from getting suspended. It remains my favorite verse in the Bible.

"Again he [Jesus] stooped down and wrote on the ground" (John 8:8). What did He write? Although Scripture doesn't say, tradition has it that Jesus exposed the accusers by writing their sins in the sand. There is some evidence for this interpretation in the Greek text as the word used in this case is *katagraphein*, which means "to write a record against someone."

"At this, those who heard began to go away one at a time, the older ones first, until only Jesus was left, with the woman still standing there. Jesus straightened up and asked her, 'Woman, where are they? Has no one condemned you?'

" 'No one, sir,' she said.

" 'Then neither do I condemn you,' Jesus declared. 'Go now and leave your life of sin' " (verses 9–11).

Jesus connected with this woman in a supernatural way. Consequently, He changed her life. Building community has a way of doing that. You, too, can build up this kind of community. How? Of the many take-homes we could pull from this classic story, let me suggest three.

1. EMBRACE ALL PEOPLE

The church leaders had no time for the prostitute. But she really mattered to Jesus. He connected with her and treated her with dignity—because all people, even the riffraff, matter to the Father. If you want to be a community-builder, treat all people with dignity and respect.

One day I had an interruption in my schedule that forced me to go to the gym a couple hours later than usual. When I arrived, my basketball buddies were not there. Instead, the gym was swarming with teenagers from the local high school. Have you hung out with high-school kids lately?

I was appalled. They used foul language. They reeked of cigarette smoke. They dressed like freaks—purple hair, nose rings. One kid had *four* earrings in one ear! I thought, *This club needs to be more careful about who they allow to join.*

That evening my telephone rang. An unknown voice questioned, "Do you know where your wallet is?"

"Huh? Well of course I know where . . ." I searched my pockets then surrendered. "Uh, . . . do *you* know where my wallet is? And who are you?"

"Yeah, I found it in the parking lot at the gym."

We agreed to meet at Blockbuster Video. When I drove into the parking lot, I had no trouble identifying the person with my wallet. It was the kid with the purple hair and four earrings.

"Thank you!" I gushed. "This is my calendar, my credit cards, my cash, my life!"

"No problem." He shrugged.

"No really, you have no idea how much this means to me. Please let me give you a gift for your help."

"No, thanks."

"But I want to give you something for your time and gas and . . ."

"No way!" he barked firmly. "I could never take your money for doing what's right."

In that instant I felt one of those Holy Spirit "hammers" when God reminds me, "Oh, be careful how you judge people. Because every person—purple hair, green hair, no hair—every person matters to the Father."

If the church is to experience the community of Christ, we must value *all* people. We dare not just love when convenient, as the Pharisees did.

2. SEE PEOPLE THROUGH GOD'S EYES

The manner in which Jesus addresses this woman ("Woman," verse 10) suggests that He really knows her. It's similar to the way He would affectionately and respectfully address His own mother (see John 19:26).

In our impersonal society these days, such gestures are rare—in spite of heroic efforts on the part of some companies to make us believe otherwise.

Recently I got a piece of junk mail. On the outside in bold type was the message: "AT LAST! KARL HAFFNER, WE'VE DESIGNED A VISA CARD ESPECIALLY DESIGNED FOR ACTIVE WOMEN JUST LIKE YOURSELF!" I assume that bank doesn't really know me. But Jesus knew this woman. He saw her as a beloved child of His Father.

I love the old story of the Christian professor at a secular university who often tried to incorporate his religious beliefs into his lectures. Since it was a state school, he couldn't blatantly teach Christian doctrines, but on occasion he could blend Christian ideology into the lectures. One afternoon he proposed the question, "How would history's thought leaders have responded to a prostitute?" The question promised some intriguing discussion.

"What would Aristotle have said when encountering a prostitute?" the professor probed. The students debated until the teacher interrupted. "How about Mohammed?" Then he asked about Buddha. At last he asked the question he really wanted to discuss: "If Jesus saw a prostitute, what would He have said to her?"

A student's hand shot up. "We'll never know, because Jesus never saw a prostitute."

"Now wait a minute," the professor replied. "John, chapter 8, records an incident when Jesus did see a prostitute."

"Not true," the student said.

"It's in the Bible," the professor insisted. "The Pharisees dragged a prostitute and dumped her at the feet of Jesus."

The student replied, "Professor, I am well aware of that story in the Bible. But do you think when Jesus saw that woman, He really saw a prostitute?"

Of course not; Jesus saw a valued child of God. So why not see people in the same way? Put on "God goggles" and revel in the value of every child of the King.

3. SHOW COMPASSION RATHER THAN CONDEMNATION

The church leaders were quick to condemn this woman, but Jesus treated her with compassion instead. In doing this, Jesus touched this woman's soul. Ellen White offers this insight:

> Her heart was melted, and she cast herself at the feet of Jesus, sobbing out her grateful love, and with bitter tears confessing her sins.
>
> This was to her the beginning of a new life, a life of purity and peace, devoted to the service of God. . . . This penitent woman became one of His most steadfast followers. With self-sacrificing love and devotion she repaid His forgiving mercy.
>
> In His act of pardoning this woman and encouraging her to live a better life, the character of Jesus shines forth in the beauty of perfect righteousness. While He does not palliate sin, nor lessen the sense of guilt, He seeks not to condemn, but to save. The world had for this erring woman only contempt and scorn; but Jesus speaks words of comfort and hope. The Sinless One pities the weakness of the sinner, and reaches to her a helping hand. While the hypocritical Pharisees denounce, Jesus bids her, "Go, and sin no more."[3]

Lest you fear that Jesus is soft on sin in this story, note that this prostitute became one of His most devoted disciples.

Compassion has the power to change a person in the deepest part of the soul. People don't soon forget such loving acts of grace.

The story of an elderly couple comes to mind. She was in the advanced stages of Alzheimer's. He lived alone at home, but every day he would visit his wife of fifty-four years.

In an effort to stimulate her memory, he quizzed her with pictures he took from the mantle at home. One day, he brought a picture of their son and asked, "Do you know who this is?"

She stared. Finally, she had to admit, "No, I don't know."

"Sweetheart," he said, "that's our boy Josh. You remember Josh, right?"

"Oooh," she replied blankly.

Taking another picture, he queried again, "Do you know who she is?"

"No."

"This is our niece. Do you remember Shari?"

"No."

Finally, he looked her in the eyes and asked, "What about me? Do you know who I am?"

After a long pause, a sliver of recognition seemed to dawn. "Yes . . . yes . . ." she said, obviously reaching for the name but unable to nail it. Finally she replied, "Yes, you're the one who loves me."

She couldn't remember his name. But she couldn't forget his love. Such is the power of compassion.

Go now, and do likewise.

The Gospel of Getting Stoned
(Questions for Reflection or Group Study)

1. Did you ever get into any mischief when you were in high school? What happened?

2. Discuss the connection between community and soul.
3. If you had been in the crowd when they dragged the woman to Jesus, what would you have done?
4. Why is it that more people confess their sins to a bartender than to a minister?
5. What is the strongest motivation for you to live a pure life?
6. Who is the most accepting person you know? What can that person teach you about acceptance?
7. The author offers three of many possible "take-homes" from the story. Make a list of other points where the story could be applied to your life.
8. Have you ever misjudged someone? What did that experience teach you?
9. If you were to see others as God sees them, in what ways might your relationships change?
10. Share a story of a time when you were on the receiving end of compassion.

---

1. As reported in *Bible Illustrator,* "Marriage," Index 1620, 1621.
2. William Barclay, *The Gospel of John,* volume 2, Revised Edition (Philadelphia: The Westminster Press, 1975), p. 2.
3. Ellen White, *The Desire of Ages,* p. 462.

—Chapter nine—
A Marriage
Made in Heaven

Dearly beloved, we gather today to witness the union of a bride and a bridegroom. By this exchange of solemn vows, you are invited to participate in the joining together of the Bridegroom and His beloved bride. This is a lifelong pledge of love, trust, and commitment. What God will join together today, let no man put asunder.

I love weddings! My favorite part of being a pastor is officiating at weddings. Even when I mess them up, I love weddings. For example, at my first wedding, the bride requested that I tell her, "You may now kiss the groom," rather than instructing him to kiss the bride. When that part of the service came I was thinking "groom," but I'm programmed to say "bride" and somehow I married the words and said, "Michelle, you may now kiss your broom!"

Even when I mess them up, I love weddings. So let's have a wedding right now, what do you say?

THE HOMILY

Intimacy was God's answer for the despondent soul. Authentic, life-giving, Christian relationships combat soul fatigue like nothing else. Some couples experience this kind of supernatural connection in their marriage. For others, this community comes in clubs or in the workplace. For all of us, it was in God's design that we find this intimacy in His church. That's why God invites you to this wedding ceremony.

Our ceremony begins by considering the Word of the

Lord for this solemn occasion. Ephesians 5:25–32 offers this counsel:

> Husbands, love your wives, as Christ loved the church and gave himself up for her, that he might sanctify her, having cleansed her by the washing of water with the word, that the church might be presented before him in splendor, without spot or wrinkle or any such thing, that she might be holy and without blemish. Even so husbands should love their wives as their own bodies. He who loves his wife loves himself. For no man ever hates his own flesh, but nourishes and cherishes it, just as Christ does the church, because we are members of his body. "For this reason a man shall leave his father and mother and be joined to his wife, and the two shall become one." This is a great mystery, and I take it to mean Christ and the church (RSV).

This text provides a portrait of God's love for His church. We see that He is so committed to the church that "He gave Himself up" for it. Also notice that this passage concludes by quoting Genesis 2, which describes what happens in a marriage—a man and a wife become one flesh. Then Paul claims that the Genesis story is actually referring to the union of Christ with His church. For God so loved His church that He gave His only begotten Son in order to redeem it. That's the intensity of the love that we're talking about here.

Joshua Harris, in his book *Stop Dating the Church,* writes "God invented romance and pursuit and the promise of undying love between a man and a woman so that throughout our lives we could catch a faint glimmer of the intense love Christ has for those He died to save. What passion He has for His Church! Even if you've never studied the Bible, you've heard the echoes of this amazing love throughout your life. Every true love story has hinted at it. Every groom weakened at the sight of his radiant bride has whispered of it. Every faithful, committed, and loving marriage has pointed to it. Each is an imperfect echo of the perfect love song of heaven."[1]

Bottle up all the love, twitterpation, and passion of a wedding and you begin to get a picture of the way God feels about His church. So please join me as we consider the participants at a typical wedding.

THE WEDDING PARTY

We begin with the bride. Everybody knows you can't have a wedding without the bride. She is the central figure of any wedding. That's why there are dozens of magazines devoted to the bride. There is *Modern Bride, Bride's, Bridal Guide, Today's Bride, Elegant Bride*—there's even a magazine called *Bride Again,* for "encore brides." But one magazine you won't find on the shelf at Borders is *Elegant Groom,* because, frankly, nobody gives a wad of chewed gum what the groom looks like. It's all about the bride.

I shall never forget the day the lobby doors opened at the Walla Walla City Church on September 7, 1986. In that moment my heart froze as I beheld for the first time my bride adorned in her wedding gown. The music soared. All heads turned as Cherié gracefully floated down the aisle beside her father. On this day, she was the star. She could do no wrong.

She tried. You see, the only request I had ever made regarding the wedding was that we do nothing except say "I do." On numerous occasions I complained to Cherié about brides and grooms who sing or speak at their own wedding. It always seems a disaster. Any lovebird getting married is too shaky to hold a note. And while it's a nice sentiment to write a love song for the betrothed, let's face it, the lyrics always sound like some kindergarten ditty: "I love you, I love you, I love you, this is true, I'm not blue, you can't go moo, I love you . . ." OK, I'm a little cynical.

After many conversations to that effect I thought Cherié and I had a clear understanding come "I do" day. You can imagine my shock when in the middle of our ceremony Cherié grabbed a microphone.

"What is going on?" I whispered to her in pure panic.

The piano player provided a short introduction, and Cherié's melodious and sure voice carried the day. She sang without a hiccup, "Father let me be his sunshine when the day is dark and drear . . ."

Whenever we're hurting for a laugh in our house we just pull out the video of that moment and watch the horrified expression on my face as I fidget and fuss all through the song. But I will admit, she sounded better than Celine. Cherié knew that she could do no wrong because it was her day. The wedding is all about the bride.

The church is Christ's bride. That's you and me. The same fondness that a groom has toward his bride God feels toward you. Do you have any idea how important you are to God?

Perhaps you've heard the story of the Irish priest who was traveling the countryside when he happened upon an old peasant sitting by the side of the road; he was just sitting there. When the priest got closer he realized that the peasant was praying, and the priest was impressed. He said to the peasant, "You must be quite close to God."

The peasant looked up from his prayer, thought for a moment, and responded, "Yes, He is very fond of me."

Do you have any idea how fond God is of you? How fond He is of His church? You are His bride, and there is no one more precious to Him.

Moving down our list of the wedding party, we always find a groom. Scripture teaches that the groom is Christ. He is perfect in every way, which begs the question: How can He accept a bride so faulty and flawed as the church? Let's be honest here, every church I know of is packed with perverts, hypocrites, liars, and vegetarians who eat people. What did we ever do to deserve this Groom?

When I think about Christ as the Groom for us, His church, I relate to the story that Joni Eareckson Tada tells of her wedding day. She was paralyzed in a diving accident as a teenager. She remembers her big day like this:

> I felt awkward as my girlfriends strained to shift my paralyzed body into a cumbersome wedding gown. No amount of corseting and binding my body gave me a perfect shape. The dress just didn't fit well. Then, as I was wheeling into the church, I glanced down and noticed that I'd accidentally run over the hem of my dress, leaving a greasy tire mark. My paralyzed hands couldn't hold the bouquet of daisies that lay off-center on my lap. And my chair, though decorated for the wedding, was still a big, clunky gray machine with belts, gears, and ball bearings. I certainly didn't feel like the picture-perfect bride in a bridal magazine.
>
> I inched my chair closer to the last pew to catch a glimpse of Ken in front. There he was, standing tall and stately in his formal attire. I saw him looking for me, craning his neck to look up the aisle. My face flushed, and I suddenly couldn't wait to be with him. I had seen my beloved. The love in Ken's face had washed away all my feelings of unworthiness. I was his pure and perfect bride.[2]

Therein is the reason for being involved in Christ's church. He is the Groom. We commit to the church because we love Jesus Christ, our pure and perfect Groom. We are not perfect. The tuxedo, the wedding gown, is plastered with spots and wrinkles. Every one of us brings a portfolio of imperfections into the mix when we join the church. But when we see Jesus, our pure and perfect Groom, we know this is where our full affections should be.

So keep your eyes on Jesus. Whatever you do, don't fixate on your own rags. And be careful not to obsess over the spots and wrinkles of others in the wedding party. For most weddings include not only the bride and the groom but the in-laws as well. Look long enough and you might find some imperfections in them!

Recently I attended the funeral for my father-in-law, Clarence Gruesbeck. He packed eighty-one years with grace, love, and laughter. He was a great man, a beloved pastor, and an exemplary father. Really, I have only one mark against the man—he paused way too long when I asked to marry his daughter.

"Um, ah, Dr. Gruesbeck," I stammered, "I, ah, as you know, I dare about your caughter—uh, that is, I care about your daughter very much. That's why we've been dating now for over four years, and I, um, well . . ."

He stared at me like a pit bull in a bad mood.

I forged on. "So, I was wondering if, I could um, you know, maybe permanently go out with Cherié, you know, like marry her."

Silence.

I squirmed. I broke eye contact and stared at his wingtips. I grew a beard.

At last he broke the silence. "And how can I know that you will take care of my little girl?"

I wasn't expecting that question on the test. I never studied for that one. In a panic I popped off the only answer that came to mind. "Well, sir, when I was a kid I took care of my dog Dusty for four years . . . before he got hit by a truck."

Somehow I knew that wasn't the right answer.

Long pause. Followed by a longer pause.

He softened a stitch and consented to give his blessing to the union. Then he said, "You know, Karl, when you marry Cherié, you're really marrying her whole family."

On that count he was right. I do spend a lot of time with Cherié's family. Luckily, they're fine folk, and we get along great—as long as we avoid topics like Krispy Kreme donuts. (My brother-in-law, Brandon, thinks they are the greatest thing since sliced bread. I've never felt that slicing bread was all that world-shattering, and I maintain that if I snuck a donut from Safeway into a Krispy Kreme box, Brandon would never know the difference. He'd still carry on about the sugar bomb "meeeeeelting in my mouth . . .")

But even if Cherié's family were a tribe of murderous, head-hunting New York Yankees fans (remember, I grew up around Boston), I'd have married her still. For you see, it's the relationship with Cherié that matters.

I point this out because too many folk bail on church because they tire of the hypocrites who occupy the pews.

"So-and-so destroyed my reputation."

"The meanest people I've met were in that church."

"All those church people cared about was getting my money."

I won't deny it. The church is composed of some real jerks. And frankly I think we do ourselves a disservice when we try to convince people to join under the pretense that "The church has changed. The people are not as legalistic as they used to be. We model 'grace' now."

Maybe. Maybe not.

While there are many wonderful people in the church, please don't join because you hope the saints have cleaned up their act. We can still be as prickly as ever. Sometimes we're about as much fun as asking a father for his daughter's hand in marriage.

Of course the church can be a wonderful, caring community. When my father-in-law died, I saw the church at its finest. Members stuffed our fridge with food, our mailbox with sympathy cards, and our answering machine with messages of support.

But nice or not, the church is just the in-laws. There's only one reason to be a part of the church, and that is to be with Christ, the Bridegroom. When you love Jesus, and you understand how much Jesus loves His church, then you'll love what Jesus loves. Thus a commitment to the local church is really a vow to Christ and to the community He established with His own blood.

Finally, to complete any wedding party you must have attendees. Many people see their involvement in church like attending a wedding. If it's convenient, they go; if it's not, they opt to do something else. That's the mentality of many when it comes to church. Church is just one of several options available on Sabbath morning. Play video games on the computer, go four-wheeling in the mountains, sleep in, or go to church? Whatever strikes my fancy on any given Sabbath is what I do.

Now imagine that attitude on my wedding day: "Oh yeah, Cherié, I intend to come to the wedding—as long as my buddies and I are done golfing. Now if some of the boys want to go out to Dairy Queen after the round, I'll be a little late or perhaps I'll skip it altogether." Had I tried that speech, I'd be a single man.

I suspect Cherié's response would have been just as cold had I told her, "I have lots of friends getting married today, so

I'll just wait and see which wedding I decide to attend. I hear the Livingstons have a great preacher officiating at their wedding, so I may go to that service. Or the Ungers have some hot music planned for their wedding, maybe I'll go there."

I could have used that excuse because we had several friends who got married on the same day that we chose. In fact, the first church where I served as pastor consisted of only fifty people, yet four couples in that church had been married on the same day—September 7, 1986. I could have attended three other weddings of friends on that day, but I wisely opted to attend my own wedding. To do otherwise never crossed my lovesick mind.

And yet how many people approach church with a similar attitude? "I'm going to First Church today because they have a funny preacher. Next week I'm going to Main Street Fellowship because they have a hot worship band." The result? We're raising a generation of twitterpation junkies that scurry to the most electric worship one week and then to the most titillating preacher the next week, never anchoring to any local church. They whine and whine of how the church fails to meet their needs—as if the church exists to cater to every entertainment whim and each emotional craving of narcissistic consumers. Heaven forbid!

Arthur Boers writes, "I often visit newcomers in town and find them to be church shopping. They want to know what they can get out of church. Churches are one more consumer commodity. Worship services are not a place for us to serve God and neighbor but a place where people expect to purchase the best: inspiring worship, good music, moving sermons, quality child care. As if we buy God and not vice versa."[3]

We are not called to be consumers in church but rather communers. We come to church to commune with God. He is the Bridegroom—which makes the church like a marriage commitment. Oh, how the church is hungry for serious followers of Christ who understand this and will commit to the church as they would to a marriage partner!

Enough of the casual commitment when it comes to church! Paul Harvey shared the true story of a woman who exemplifies this kind of commitment. She called the Butterball Turkey Company hotline that was set up to answer consumer questions about preparing turkeys. This woman wanted some answers to questions she had about cooking a turkey that had been in the bottom of her freezer for twenty-three years. That's right—twenty-three years! The Butterball representative told her the turkey would probably be safe to eat if the freezer had been kept below zero for the entire twenty-three years. But the Butterball representative warned her that even if the turkey was safe to eat, the flavor would probably have deteriorated to such a degree that she wouldn't recommend eating it.

The caller replied, "That's what I thought. We'll give the turkey to our church."[4]

It's time to talk turkey about the church. We must stop giving our musty seconds to the church and elevate the bride of Jesus to its rightful place in our lives. It's time to show the same kind of commitment to the church that Christ has made. It's time for the vows.

THE VOWS

Boil it down, and what makes a wedding a wedding? There are a lot of things we associate with weddings. Take, for example, expensive clothes. A bride wears a dress that costs about as much as a submarine. Then the bridesmaids rack up a fortune on their gowns. Of course, every bride tells her bridesmaids, "This time the bridesmaids' dresses will be really nice. You can wear them to other events." But they never do. They always look dorky. Even the groom plunks down a lot of cash for his clothes. But you could do a wedding without expensive clothes.

Most weddings have flower girls, Bible boys, candles, cake, and guest books. But none of that stuff is essential. But what about the vows? Ironically, couples often invest more in every detail of the wedding except the most important part—the vows. And yet, that's what the wedding is—a promise offered, a promise received, a promise witnessed, a promise kept. It's a promise to stay together until the very end. Without that promise, you can't have a wedding.

Walter Wangerin puts it like this:

> Marriage begins when two people make the clear, unqualified promise to be faithful, each to the other, until the end of their days. That spoken promise makes the difference. . . .
>
> A promise made, a promise witnessed, a promise heard, remembered, trusted—this is the groundwork of marriage. Not emotions. No, not even love. Not physical desires or personal needs or sexuality. Not the practical fact of living together. Not even the piercing foresight or some peculiar miracle of All-seeing God. Rather, a promise, a vow, makes the marriage.[5]

That's what makes the wedding such a sobering and significant occasion. It's a nothing-held-back promise, " 'Til death do us part."

That's the metaphor that Scripture gives us of the church. So now it's time to commit to the church with the same " 'til death do us part" intensity that Christ showed toward His bride.

When cruel death gripped Christ on the cross, all of creation froze. Would the Son of God make the ultimate commitment to redeem humankind? And from that crimson beam Jesus screamed in anguish His answer: "I do." That's the commitment He made to His bride, His church. Will you do the same?

If you want to respond in kind to Christ, then prayerfully answer this vow:

Wilt thou have this Bridegroom, Jesus Christ, to be thy spiritually wedded Soulmate? To live together after God's ordinance in the sacred estate of His church? Wilt thou commit to serving in His church? To attending regularly? To using thy gifts in whatever way possible to build up His church? Wilt thou love, honor, and cherish your Bridegroom by committing to His church, in sickness and in health, in prosperity or adversity; and, forsaking all other distractions, keep thyself only unto this Bridegroom so long as ye shall live? Do you so declare?

A Marriage Made in Heaven
(Questions for Reflection or Group Study)

1. Tell a wedding story.
2. Share your spiritual upbringing and your involvement in church.
3. What other metaphors (besides marriage) might be used to describe the church?
4. How does the relationship between Christ and the church explain the role of the partners in a marriage?
5. What role can the church play in nurturing your soul?
6. What is your most difficult challenge in committing yourself more to the local church? Why do you think

many people are so casual in their commitments to the local church?

7. How do you react when you read of your church being "packed with perverts, hypocrites, liars, and cheats"?

8. Do you think that in recent times there has been a shift within the church away from legalism and toward grace? What are the dangers of erring on either side?

9. Write your own vows to the Bridegroom.

---

1. Joshua Harris, *Stop Dating the Church* (Sisters, Ore.: Multnomah Publishers).

2. John H. Akers, John H. Armstrong, and John D. Woodbridge, eds., *This We Believe: The Good News of Jesus Christ for the World* (Grand Rapids, Mich.: Zondervan Publishing House, 2000), p. 222.

3. Arthur Boers, "The Other Side," *Christianity Today,* vol. 33, no. 11, (May/June 1989).

4. Paul Harvey, daily radio broadcast (November 22, 1995).

5. Walter Wangerin, Jr., *As for Me and My House* (Thomas Nelson Publishers, 1987) as quoted at, < http://www.reformedworship.org/cprw_rw59_covenant.htm >.

Soul Goodness

"True religion is real living;

living with all one's soul,

with all one's goodness

and righteousness."

(Albert Einstein, 1879–1955)

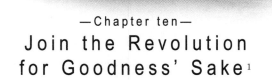

Chapter ten

Join the Revolution
for Goodness' Sake[1]

I've always thought it would be cool to start my own revolution.

I've had this craving since graduation weekend my senior year in high school when, for class night, I played the role of Patrick Henry. After donning a white wig and some goofy looking wool breeches, I took the stage and recited the immortal words: "They tell us, sir, that we are weak; unable to cope with so formidable an adversary. But when shall we be stronger? . . . Is life so dear, or peace so sweet, as to be purchased at the price of chains and slavery? Forbid it, Almighty God! I know not what course others may take; but as for me, give me liberty or give me death!"

Wow! Talk about the rush of the revolution! There's nothing better for the soul than embracing a cause worth dying for.

So now I'm on the warpath again. Only this time I'm calling for a revolution of goodness. Jesus planted the seeds of this revolt during a conversation with a rich young ruler. Mark 10:17, 18 records,

> As Jesus started on his way, a man ran up to him and fell on his knees before him. "Good teacher," he asked, "what must I do to inherit eternal life?"
>
> "Why do you call me good?" Jesus answered. "No one is good—except God alone."

What's striking about this conversation is that Jesus stops

the man and makes a big issue about being called "Good teacher." Why such a fuss? After all, in previous conversations Jesus never balked at titles such as "Son of God," "Son of David," or even "Messiah." But in this case He takes the man to task over a seemingly benign title about being "good."

Jesus' reaction no doubt startled the young man. He had addressed Jesus as one would greet any rabbi in that day. It was a throw-away comment much like people who say to me on their way out of church, "Good sermon, Pastor." This compliment used to mean a lot to me until one week after church three different people said, "Good sermon, Pastor." The only problem: I didn't preach that morning! I realized then that people feel compelled to say *something,* but in reality they're not paying close enough attention to even notice who is preaching! It's a throw-away quip, much like this man uses to address Jesus. And yet Jesus stops him to say, "No one is good—except God alone."

In this response, we are reminded of two important principles that are especially relevant in our postmodern era of relativism. First, Jesus reminds us that there is in fact a standard of goodness. In other words, there is black and white, right and wrong, good and bad.

These days it's politically incorrect to suggest that any standard of goodness actually exists—but it's still true. These days, no one dares to say the word *carrot* for fear of offending carb-counters. And I'm not "bald" anymore; I'm "comb free." Also, please drop the word *roadkill* from your vocabulary; now it's "vehicularly compressed maladaptive life forms."

If we're going to launch a revolution, we must be willing to buck the status quo. Frankly I get tired of "pansy footing" around people who feel called to call me on every sentence I write. For example, some years ago I received a toxic missive that voiced "grave concern" and called me a "bigot," a "racist," and a "white supremacist." Harsh language, don't you think? This came in response to an article I had written describing a basketball game in which I noted that all the players were black except for one short white guy who looked different from his teammates.

I honestly did not mean to disparage anyone, black or white. I was merely describing what I saw. But I should have known that you can't do that anymore without offending someone.

Jesus Himself didn't cower to political correctness. Instead He boldly proclaimed, "I am . . . the truth" (John 14:6). He didn't say "I am one of many viable truths." He said, "I am *the* truth."

Carol Tharp suggests, "Western culture has made a fundamental change in its religious base. We have exchanged that One who said, 'I am the Truth' (John 14:6) for the incredibly expensive doctrine of Freud and the words of all his varied disciples. Our new religion says with Pontius Pilate, 'What is truth?' and teaches that our status is one of 'original victim' rather than 'original Sin.' "[2]

It's so easy to buy into this bunkum and even pass it along to our kids. I'm reminded of the fourth-grader who had to be so careful to keep from offending anyone that she reported on the origins of the Thanksgiving holiday in this way: "The pilgrims came here seeking freedom of you know what. When they landed, they gave thanks to you know who. Because of them, we can worship you know where."

Enough already! For goodness' sake, it's time for a revolution. It's time to take responsibility and fully embrace truth. Edgy, offensive, politically incorrect—let the quips fall where they may. Until there is clarity on this point, the soul will flounder. Part of experiencing a soul that is fully at peace involves being clear on what is true and what is false. There *is* such a thing as sin. There *are* moral absolutes. There *is* right and wrong. And there is only *one* way to salvation—Jesus Christ. (If that offends you, write me a letter. I'll read it while I'm carbo loading on carrots.)

There is a standard of goodness. But the response of Jesus, "No one is good—except God alone," reminds us of a second truth: Goodness comes from God alone. In other words, if we're serious about this revolution of goodness, then it will happen by God dwelling within us. It will not occur by trying really hard to be good. It will take place only when God's goodness flows through us.

Too often we try to be good as if it's an assignment like keeping a hundred beach balls submerged in the Pacific Ocean at the same time. You may keep one ball under water with your feet and a couple more submerged with your hands, but soon you'll feel defeated and exhausted.

Similarly, some people think, *If I can just keep my sins like pride and gluttony and lust under the surface so others don't see them, maybe at least I'll look like I'm a good person.* That's a sure recipe for failure. Soon you will feel defeated and exhausted.

So what's the answer? Get out of the water and into the boat with Jesus. The key is not to try harder to be good; rather, it is to remain in the presence of Jesus. For sin and Jesus cannot coexist in the same heart. Your battle is to always remain in the presence of God in order to let His life be willed through you.

It's like the father who tells of watching his three-year-old daughter fight the temptation of the cookie jar. The girl doesn't notice that her father is watching from a distance. So she climbs a shelf in the pantry and stretches to snitch a snack. Now she knows the cookie jar is off limits. Her spirit wants to resist temptation, but her flesh craves a sugar hit. Just as she grabs a cookie, Dad clears his throat. Instantly she drops the cookie and scoots away.

Think about it. One moment the kid could not resist temptation, but in an instant she models the resolution of a saint. What makes the difference? Simple—it is the presence of her father.

Our struggle to be good works the same way. In our own strength, the flesh always wins, and the soul always loses. But when we live in the presence of our heavenly Father, we are then positioned to allow God to be good through us.

GOODNESS DEFINED

Following this interesting exchange that opens their dialogue, Jesus defines goodness for this rich young man:

> "You know the commandments: 'Do not murder, do not commit adultery, do not steal, do not give false testimony, do not defraud, honor your father and mother.' "
>
> "Teacher," he declared, "all these I have kept since I was a boy."
>
> Jesus looked at him and loved him. "One thing you lack," he said. "Go, sell everything you have and give to the poor, and you will have treasure in heaven. Then come, follow me."
>
> At this the man's face fell. He went away sad, because he had great wealth (Mark 10:19–22).

The man aspired to be good, but he didn't want to be *that* good.

Jesus reminds us of the radical nature of revolutions. To sell everything you have and give it to the poor is not easy or convenient. It's more than just flipping a quarter to a homeless man on Main Street. No wonder Jesus went on to explain, " 'It is easier for a camel to go through the eye of a needle than for a rich man to enter the kingdom of God' " (verse 25).

Perhaps you've heard some of the interpretations of this text that help to ease the extreme flavor of the statement. For example, maybe you've heard someone explain this verse by saying that in Jerusalem there was an entrance called the "needle gate." It was very narrow, and the only way a camel could squeeze through it was to get down on its knees. Thus, what Jesus was really saying is that it's OK to hoard money as long as you do it on your knees, in the spirit of prayer. It's a sweet explanation—except it's not true. There was no such gate in Jerusalem. The story probably came from a rich guy looking for a loophole from the implications of what Jesus is saying.

Another explanation is that Jesus was really saying to the young ruler that his wealth was not under God's stewardship. If only this man would have acknowledged that everything he owned belonged to God, he could have kept his possessions.

I've always wondered if what Jesus really meant when He said, "Go, sell everything, and give it to the poor," was, "Go, sell everything, and give it to the poor."

Revolutions are that radical. Revolutions happen when one Patrick Henry or one Rosa Parks or one Martin Luther declares, "Herein is a cause worth dying for. I will give my very life to advance this cause."

I've heard about a group of philanthropists in Chicago who meet regularly to decide how they will give away their resources. They call themselves The Bruised Camels. They understand that for a camel to fit through the eye of a needle it's going to be uncomfortable for the camel. And if they take Jesus seriously, they will get bruised. You see, when people get serious about the revolution for goodness' sake, the result will be some "bruised camels."

Perry Bigelow is a bruised camel. He was the owner of a twenty-million-dollar construction business. He lived in a six-bedroom home that offered a stunning view of the Chicago skyline. He schmoozed with the city's elite and wielded great power, but he felt increasingly uncomfortable with his life due to a personal conviction of the importance of serving the poor in the inner city.

So Perry Bigelow walked away from his dynasty. He moved into a crumbling tenement in one of Chicago's most ravaged West Side neighborhoods. Now he lives in a ten-foot by twelve-foot room that features a view of a boarded-up building and a vacant trash-dotted lot across the street. He devotes his time to helping people build their own homes in the inner city. A reporter asked Perry Bigelow, "So why did you move in? It's one thing to offer people some help. But why did you move in?"

"Well," he said, "I didn't know any poor people, and Jesus did."

Follow the counsel of Jesus, and you just might get bruised. Your portfolio may get drained. Your comfort may be compromised. You may be called to move to a dumpy neighborhood. Your faith may be tested. But understand: It's in the revolution that you experience the adventure of the kingdom. By selling out, your soul will be fully satisfied.

Some years ago I enjoyed an evening of ropin', ridin', buckin', and bustin'—mutton bustin' that is. The idea of mutton bustin' is basic: Parents (who have the intelligence of rope) let their kids mount sheep that gallop around like rabid bulls wearing wool sweaters. When the sheep explodes out of the fence, cowboys leap to their feet and shout things like: "Ride 'er low Joey-Jim-Jerry-Johnny-Bob!"

My first exposure to the sport came when I received some free tickets to the Rooftop PRCA Rodeo in Estes Park, Colorado. I stared in disbelief as child after child bit the dirt—much to the delight of people whom Jeff Foxworthy talks about a lot.

I remember one incident especially well. A sheep named Satan's Sidekick bolted out of the gate with its rider, seven-year-old Shannon Williams from Pueblo, Colorado. She was clutching fleece and catching some "face peal" in the wind. The animal was doing about Mach 10 when it rammed Shannon into a fence. She dropped like a duck sniped out of the air. Everyone gasped. We sat motionless while the child lay momentarily paralyzed. Paramedics scurried to scene.

To no one in particular, I asked incredulously, "What parent in their right mind would let their kid do that?" Only after my question escaped my big mouth did I notice that the woman next to me was looking down—as if in prayer. She snapped out of her vigil long enough to look up at me and announce, "That's my daughter!"

I felt like the star of a Southwest Airlines commercial— "Need to get away?" I excused myself and escaped to the popcorn stand under the bleachers. As I walked down the stairs, Shannon bounced to her feet and walked unassisted out of the corral. The audience erupted in applause.

The tinny speakers crackled, "Good news! She's OK folks. How about another round of applause for Shannon Williams?"

I camped at the popcorn stand just long enough to, well, retire. I kept spying on the mom, hoping she'd leave. But she proved to be as permanent as a judge in the Supreme Court. I would have just left, but I needed to return to my seat to retrieve my valuables, namely my wife and daughter.

Resigning myself to the inevitable, I sheepishly (pun intended) returned to sit next to the woman and her daughter, Shannon.

My fears of awkward silence quickly evaporated as the kid was keen to tell everyone within earshot of her experience. "It was great!" she bubbled. "There's nuttin' better! I hit the wall, and the whole world looked this big." She gestured a small circle with her thumb and finger. "Then I realized I was staring through the ear hole in my helmet! Mom, can I do it again?"

After all that, can you believe she wanted to give it another shot? Of course! Why? Because life is more fun when you get out of the stands and onto the field. Listen to Lloyd Ogilve:

> Our spectator culture is profoundly challenged by the gospel of a God of grace who acts in the arena of human history. Today we are so used to watching— before the TV set, at the ball game, even in the worship service. We become expert analysts of the action replay, brilliant strategists, great talkers; but all from the comfort of our spectator's seat. We have lost the thrill of being in the rough and tumble, amidst the ups and downs of the team commitment to put things together and achieving results against the odds. We forget what it is like to be on the inside, with all its heartache but with its exultation too. Our highs and lows are experienced vicariously. We are shadows of our real selves.[3]

Don't be a shadow. Get in the game. You may get bloody and bruised, but that's the only way to experience the rush of the revolution, for goodness' sake.

BE GOOD

Our world today tends to be quite casual about a calling to goodness. Ask someone, "How was the restaurant?"

"Good," the person replies. In other words, it wasn't great, but it was OK. We read books like *From Good to Great.*

But not everyone takes this calling to goodness so casually. I think of Eva Hart, a survivor on the *Titanic.* When asked about that fateful night, Eva could recount the details. She was seven years old. Her father's last words as he lowered her into the lifeboat were stark and simple: "Be a good girl," he said.[4] She never saw him again. Throughout her long life she was guided by her dad's parting words. Every day she strived to be a good girl; she tried to live a life worthy of her father's sacrifice.

Her story is similar to ours. We, too, have been saved by our Father's sacrifice. And from the bloody cross Jesus calls us to lives of goodness. He tells us, "Live a life that was worth saving."

I know not what course others may take; but as for me, give me goodness or give me death! Now there you have a cause worth dying for. So join the revolution for goodness' sake!

Join the Revolution for Goodness' Sake
(Questions for Reflection or Group Study)

1. If you could be any revolutionary in history (Martin Luther, Patrick Henry, Martin Luther King, Jr., Hugh Hefner, etc.), whom would it be and why?
2. How comfortable are you with the assertion that there is such a thing as absolute truth?
3. Do you tend to err on the one side of being too politically correct or on the other side of being too blunt and honest? Share a personal story to illustrate.
4. "If we're going to launch a revolution, we must be willing to buck the status quo." What "status quo" in our world do you think is most in need of being challenged?
5. How do you reconcile your possessions with Jesus' command to sell everything and give it to the poor? Discuss how God relates to the wealthy.

6. Do you know of any bruised camels? Who? What qualifies them as bruised camels?

7. Describe a risk you took that has paid off for you. Are there any risks you regret? Why?

8. What part of the story of the rich young ruler do you relate to the most? Explain.

9. How can you be a part of the goodness revolution today?

1. I am indebted for the inspiration of this chapter and some of the Bible commentary on this passage to the sermon manuscript of John Ortberg, "The Fruit of the Spirit: Goodness," as found at <http://www.mppc.org/esermons.html?next_page=4&curr_page=3>.

2. Carol Tharp in a letter to the *Chicago Tribune Magazine* (April 17, 1994). *Christianity Today*, vol. 38, no. 7, as quoted at <http://www.nnedaog.org/sermons/SERIAM7.HTM>.

3. Lloyd Ogilve, "The Storm before the Calm" at <http://www.gvyouth.org/documents/sermons/The_Storm_before_the_Calm.doc>.

4. Quoted on <http://www2.nexus.edu.au/Teachstud/titanic2/media/media94.htm>.

—Chapter eleven—

I'm the Servant Leader Around Here . . . So Buck Up and Follow!

Robert Greenleaf created quite the buzz in the business community when he developed his theory of "servant leadership" back in 1970. Leaders are still quite enamored with his ideas. While many leaders give lip service to "servant leadership," rarely do we see it in real life.

Occasionally, however, a servant-leader comes along who descends into greatness. Jane Byrne comes to mind. She was the mayor of Chicago who made a highly publicized tour of Cabrini-Green. This public housing project of eighty-one high rises and row houses embodied evil in its purest form. Gangs controlled the fourteen thousand people living there. Rape, murder, extortion, drugs, and violence—these vices riddled the residents on a daily basis.

Addressing the terrorized citizens, the mayor promised, "You are going to live in security and safety." It sounded like a typical promise from a polished politician. That is, until the next week when Ms. Byrne announced her plans to leave her luxury apartment and move to Cabrini-Green! Now that raised some eyebrows. Headlines screamed, MAYOR MOVING TO CABRINI! Commented one city politician, "It is a pretty dramatic thing to do."[1]

Indeed, servant leadership is dramatic. As dramatic as the mayor moving might be, it pales in comparison to the Son of God taking up residence in our unruly world. And yet, that is exactly what Jesus did. Then He taught the guts of servant leadership when He said, "Whoever wants to be a leader among you must be your servant, and whoever wants to be first must become your slave" (Matthew 20:26, 27, NLT).

My hunch is that nobody would quarrel with the tenets of servant leadership. Who would dare disregard the clear counsel of Christ? And yet, in practice, the prevailing attitude of Christian leaders often sounds more like this: "I'm the servant leader around here . . . now buck up and follow!"

So do you aspire to servant leadership?

Really?

Whether you're the CEO of a Fortune 500 company or a stay-at-home dad, Jesus calls you to be a servant. And when you truly serve, from a selfless heart, your soul is shaped in deep and significant ways. Whether you're leading a workforce or your family, you will have plenty of opportunities today to let those around you know that you are a servant.

How? Let me be specific by underscoring the major themes from the book of James. This classic letter, penned by the half-brother of Jesus, could be considered the definitive training manual for servant leaders. Here are four suggestions from James:

1. PRACTICE SERVANT LEADERSHIP WITH YOUR EYES

This might be called the ministry of noticing. James 2:15, 16 puts it like this: "Suppose a brother or sister is without clothes and daily food. If one of you says to him, 'Go, I wish you well; keep warm and well fed,' but does nothing about his physical needs, what good is it?"

If it wasn't so tragic it would almost be comical. Imagine, James suggests, approaching someone who is starving and naked to say, "Hope you enjoy watching me inhale Krispy Kremes. Oh, and by the way . . . nice threads." Of what value is that? Authentic servant leaders develop eyes that notice needs.

Want to be a servant leader? Then notice the needs of people. Notice what they do right, and affirm that. It's so simple, yet powerful.

I once received a letter from my boss that basically said, "I noticed." He wrote, "Dear Karl, I noticed an article you had written in the Sabbath School Teacher's helps. I noticed that your church met its financial goals last month. I noticed . . ." He went on to say, "I don't know how you get everything done that you do, but I want you to know that somebody notices such things. I appreciate you." Then he offered this P.S.: "Enclosed you'll find a very small token of my appreciation."

Sure enough, he sent a crisp five dollar bill. Isn't that classy? I know it's not a lot of money, but imagine if everyone reading this book were to notice what I do! (You know I'm kidding. Don't—and I repeat—DON'T send me money . . . unless, of course, you're really spiritual, then by all means—I'm joking!)

The point is you can practice servant leadership by noticing what people do. Perhaps you can call your stepchild and say, "I noticed you mowed the lawn last night." Or write your boss a note: "I noticed you stayed after work again last night. That kind of commitment is inspiring to me." Or take your local police chief out to lunch to say, "I noticed the newspaper article. . . ."

2. PRACTICE SERVANT LEADERSHIP WITH YOUR EARS

This might be called the ministry of empathizing. James offers this advice to servant leaders: "My dear brothers, take note of this: Everyone should be quick to listen, slow to speak and slow to become angry" (James 1:19).

Now when James calls us to be good listeners, he is suggesting more than just hearing auditory sounds. He has in mind the notion of empathy. In other words, he wants us to be authentic servants and really crawl into the skin of someone in need.

I learned about the ministry of empathizing when my wife, Cherié, was pregnant. We dutifully enrolled in a Lamaze class. Now for the record, Lamaze tends to be quite optimistic about the whole birth deal. For example, our Swedish instructor, Natilda, would never use the word *pain* when talking about delivery. Instead, she said, "You may experience some *discomfort*." She even took us though a simulation exercise in which we clipped clothespins on our ears—as if to suggest delivering a baby would feel much the same. Then she instructed us to "think happy thoughts" in order to cope with the "discomfort." (By the way, Natilda had no children of her own.)

I, too, was assigned a role in the birth. I was to be the empathizer. "Put yourself in your wife's place," Natilda cooed. "Feeeeeeeel her discomfort. Seize the moment as if you were the deliverer. Support the one you love."

"OK," I said. "Empathy. Righto. I'll deliver!"

The day that went down in empathy finally came. Our doctor induced the baby at 8:00 A.M. This was welcome news since we assumed the ordeal would be over by noon. By noon, however, Cherié was in excruciating pain—with no promise of a munchkin anytime soon. By 6:00 P.M. Cherié was saying things I'd never heard her say before. (I discreetly closed the door in case any church members were roaming the halls.) I tried to be a good empathizer, but I felt more like a magician trying to coax a greased calf through a cat door. Nothing seemed to work (except Cherié—now *she* was working).

After twenty hours, Cherié let out a scream that turned my spine into a crystal goblet in the old Memorex commercials. So I said, "Honey, are you experiencing some discomfort?"

Come to find out, that was not the most empathetic thing I could have done. While that may go without saying, let's agree that empathy is a tricky art at best. How can I really know what it's like to have a baby? Sorry, Ms. Discomfort, but I'm not convinced by the clothespins. How can I feel the pain, the joy, the struggle, or passion of another person? It's a precarious proposition to be sure.

Nevertheless, it is possible to model empathy. Look at Jesus. He lived a sinless life, yet empathized with sinners. We do not need to experience the exact things that another is experiencing; we must primarily be willing to listen so deeply that we are consumed in the same emotions as the other person.

Empathy isn't easy, but it's worth the effort. So why not give it a whirl? Walk in someone else's Birkenstocks. Put on someone's pain. Crawl into another's skin. The dividends will be well worth the investment. For Cherié and me, the result was tons of joy—that weighed eight pounds, fourteen ounces.

3. PRACTICE SERVANT LEADERSHIP WITH YOUR MOUTH

Another way that you can be a servant leader today is by using your mouth to practice the ministry of blessing. Again, this is a prevalent theme in the book of James. "If anyone considers himself religious and yet does not keep a tight rein on his tongue, he deceives himself and his religion is worthless" (James 1:26).

Think about tongue power. On the one hand, words can wound the soul. Whoever suggested that sticks and stones can break the bones, but that words will never hurt ought to be sued for slander. Words can hurt!

But on the other hand, words can also heal. Proverbs 16:24 reminds us, "Pleasant words are a honeycomb, sweet to the soul and healing to the bones." So practice servant leadership today and venture words of affirmation, love, and blessing.

Speak kindness to your roommate, your professor, or your employees. Maybe you haven't talked to your ex-wife for years. You are so angry because of what she did to you. Well, the Holy Spirit is talking to you: "Be a servant leader. Take the initiative to humbly serve the person who least deserves your love."

4. PRACTICE SERVANT LEADERSHIP WITH YOUR HANDS

The final way that James calls us to be servant leaders is by putting our hands to work and practicing the ministry of service. "Religion that God our Father accepts as pure and faultless is this: to look after orphans and widows in their distress" (James 1:27).

According to James, servant leadership manifests itself by caring for the marginalized. My favorite story in this area comes from Philip Yancey.

It seems a woman went with her fiancé to the Hyatt Hotel in downtown Boston to arrange the details for their wedding banquet. The couple pored over the menu, selected china and silver, ordered flower arrangements, and so on. Because they had pricey tastes, the bill totaled over thirteen thousand dollars! They left a deposit and went on to tackle the seemingly endless list of other details for the big day.

Then the romance soured. The day the invitations were to be sent, the potential groom got cold feet. "I can't go through with this," he whined. "I must break off our relationship."

When the fiancée tried to cancel the banquet, the events manager at the Hyatt could not have been more sympathetic. She even shared her own story of heartache. "But about the refund," she said, "I have bad news. The contract is legally binding. You're entitled to only thirteen hundred dollars back. You have two options: Forfeit the rest of the down payment or go ahead with the banquet. I'm sorry, I really am."

It was a wild idea, but the more the jilted bride thought about it, the more she liked the idea of going ahead with the party. It wouldn't be a wedding banquet, of course, but it would be a banquet just the same.

You see, ten years before, this woman had been living in a homeless shelter. Thanks to some community servant leaders, however, she was able to get a good job and save some money. Now, she wanted to treat the down-and-outs of Boston to a night on the town.

Yancey writes:

And so it was in June of 1990 the Hyatt Hotel of downtown Boston hosted a party such as it had never seen before. The hostess changed the menu to boneless chicken—"in honor of the groom," she said—and sent invitations to rescue missions and homeless shelters. That warm summer night, people who were used to peeling half-gnawed pizza off the cardboard dined instead on chicken cordon bleu. Hyatt waiters in tuxedos served *hors d'oeuvres* to senior citizens propped up by crutches and aluminum walkers. Bag ladies, vagrants, and addicts took one night off from the hard life on the sidewalks outside and instead sipped champagne, ate chocolate wedding cake, and danced to big band melodies late into the night.[2]

Maybe this week you too can be a servant leader and throw a banquet for someone in need. It may not look like the meal Yancey describes, but just the same you can use your hands to serve people in need.

I say, enough with all the lip service about servant leadership. It's time to unleash an army of real servant leaders.

So forward march! Be a servant leader. How? With your

eyes—notice the needs of others. With your ears—hear the hurts of people around you. With your mouth—speak words of blessing. And with your hands—serve "the least of these," and you will be the greatest leader in the only kingdom that counts.

I'm the Servant Leader Around Here . . . So Buck Up and Follow!
(Questions for Reflection or Group Study)

1. What does a servant leader look like? Sound like? Act like?
2. Who first comes to mind when you hear the term "servant leader"? Why?
3. How would you summarize the book of James?
4. Reflect on the last twenty-four hours. What positive things did you see in people that you might affirm by letting them know you noticed?
5. Have you ever been on the receiving end of empathy? What happened, and how did it make you feel?
6. Tell a story of when someone shared the right words at the right time and affected you in a significant way.
7. How can you "throw a banquet" for somebody today? What things can you do to be a servant leader with your hands?

---

1. Adapted from S. Rickly Christian, *Alive* (Grand Rapids, Mich.: Zondervan Publishing House, 1990), p. 115.
2. Philip Yancey, *What's So Amazing About Grace?* (Grand Rapids, Mich.: Zondervan Publishing House, 1997), 49.

—Chapter twelve—
Go Out
Like a Light

Recently I saw a clip from the movie *About Schmidt*. Jack Nicholson stars as Warren Schmidt, a man leading a life of quiet desperation. He has retired as vice president at an insurance company, but as he reflects on his life he is plagued by the realization that it has been meaningless. Moreover, he sees his retirement as completely futile as well.

Then Warren sponsors a six-year-old orphan named Ndugu in Tanzania. He faithfully sends letters along with twenty-two dollars a month. In his letters Warren shares his inner angst:

> I know we're all pretty small in the scheme of things, and I guess the best you can hope for is to make some kind of difference. What difference have I made? What in the world is better because of me? I am weak, and I am a failure. There's just no getting around it. Real soon I will die. Maybe twenty years—maybe tomorrow—it doesn't matter. Once I am dead and everyone who knew me dies, it is as though I never existed. What difference has my life made to anyone? None that I can think of. Hope things are fine with you.
>
> Yours truly, Warren Schmidt.

The movie ends with a scene of Warren coming home to an empty house—an apt metaphor for his empty life. He enters his home with an armload of impersonal junk mail—another metaphor of his useless life. Then he spots a letter from the orphanage.

It is a letter from a nun who works where Ndugu lives. She explains that Ndugu cannot read or write, but that he thinks of Warren every day and hopes he is happy. Enclosed is a picture drawn by Ndugu for Warren—two stick people smiling and holding hands. Warren is overcome with emotion as he realizes that he has finally made a difference.

Warren is no different from you or me, is he? Deep within every human spirit is a desire to make a difference. God created us with this soul hunger for purpose. He wired every child with a desire to affect the world. Then Jesus came in person to this earth and challenged us to live on purpose.

Jesus called us to a life of purpose when He offered this challenge: "You are the light of the world," (Matthew 5:14). The word *you* is in the emphatic form. Jesus points to His followers and says "You and *only* you . . ." In other words, if God's light is going to penetrate the darkness, it will happen only through people like you and me. There is no game plan B.

Malcolm Muggeridge offers this commentary on the text: "What a stupendous phrase! And how particularly marvelous today, when one is conscious of so much darkness in the world! Let your light shine before men, he [Jesus] exhorted us. You know, sometimes . . . someone asks me what I most want, what I should most like to do in the little that remains of my life, and I always nowadays truthfully answer—and it is truthful—'I should like my light to shine, even if only very fitfully, like a match struck in a dark, cavernous night and then flickering out.' "[1]

Jesus develops this metaphor further: "A city on a hill cannot be hidden" (Matthew 5:14). Cities in ancient Palestine were typically built on hills. Because they were often constructed of white limestone, they would gleam in the sun, making them especially visible. As Jesus spoke the words on a hill above the Sea of Galilee, the listeners could look around and see the white, gleaming towns and villages that lit up the hillsides surrounding the lake.

"Neither do people light a lamp and put it under a bowl. Instead they put it on its stand, and it gives light to everyone in the house" (Matthew 5:15).

The houses in Palestine were usually dark inside with only one circular window about eighteen inches across. In order to see anything, people needed light inside. This typically came from a lamp that was a clay or metal bowl, often in the shape of a saucer, filled with oil and with a wick floating in it. When the light was extinguished, it was difficult to relight. After sunset, in order to get the most visibility, the lamp would be placed on a stand or hung from the center post of the house. So at night, from a distance, the cities on the hill would glow from the lamps shining through the window in every house.

A city on a hill cannot be hidden in day or night. Jesus' point is clear: Christianity is something that is meant to be seen. William Barclay comments: "As someone has well said, there can be no such thing as secret discipleship, for either the secrecy destroys the discipleship, or the discipleship destroys the secrecy."[2]

Secret discipleship is an oxymoron. There is no such thing. If you really understand the good news, you can't keep it to yourself. Good news is like that. It's like the TV commercial in which someone reports at the most inappropriate time, "I just saved a bunch of money on my car insurance by switching to Geico." A similar commercial has someone telling everyone, again at very inappropriate times, "I just lowered my cholesterol!"

I can relate to that commercial because I have been guilty of doing the same thing. About a year ago I caught the end of a newscast in which the reporter told of a study that showed how blueberries were just as effective as medicine at lowering cholesterol. This caught my attention since I had recently been informed that my cholesterol was 212—way too high.

So I started eating blueberries. A *lot* of blueberries. A big bowl of blueberries every morning. It helps that I love blueberries—although not as much as M&Ms.

Six months later I had my cholesterol checked. It had dropped to 156—well within the acceptable range! Since then I have been an evangelist for the blueberry. I can't help myself.

This summer I have frequented a local blueberry farm. The other day the owner told me, "Last summer we picked twenty-five thousand pounds of berries; already this summer, we've sold over sixty thousand pounds." Then she added, "I think half of that is what you have picked."

My freezer is packed with blueberries. Moreover, I have shared my blueberry story with thousands of people. Consequently, many of my friends have picked berries, and many of their friends picked berries, and many of their friends. . . .

Such is the nature of good news. You can't keep it to yourself.

Jesus then says, "In the same way, let your light shine before men, that they may see your good deeds and praise your Father in heaven" (Matthew 5:16).

Notice that as God lives in you, people notice. They see the good deeds that naturally flow out of your life, and then they praise the Father in Heaven.

On the one hand, light has so much potential for good. On the other hand, light has great potential for evil. It can be positive or negative. As Sheldon Vanauken puts it: "The best argument for Christianity is Christians: their joy, their certainty, their completeness. But the strongest argument *against* Christianity is also Christians—when they are somber and joyless, when they are self-righteous and smug in complacent consecration, when they are narrow and repressive, then Christianity dies a thousand deaths."[3]

Light can glare or it can glow.

BEING THE LIGHT

Think about light that glares. Too much light can be blinding. Have you ever met a Christian like that?

Some years ago I heard about an evangelism kit that instructed Christians how to attach a loudspeaker to their car so they could drive around and preach on the road. You've heard of drive-by shootings? This was drive-by shoutings.

The author of this book offers this advice: "The faster the car's speed, the shorter the sermon ought to be."

Really?

Then he provided some sample sermon lines. "If you see a car pulled over at a stop light, you're supposed to say, 'Pull over right now so Jesus can save your soul.' "

I'm sure this author had good motives to share Jesus, but it's too glaring if you ask me.

Ron Rearick, in his book *Iceman*, tells about using this kind of in-your-face approach. He was a Mafia strong man. His last crime was to hijack a plane for a million dollars. After meeting Christ in prison, he was miraculously released by the same judge who had sentenced him to twenty-five years. Upon his release, he set out to witness.

Thrilled by the fact that he was now "clean" from drugs, Ron had been yearning to discover just how he could become involved in "God's business." He found the address of a Christian supply store in a phone book and went right over to purchase his own supply of leaflets.

Back in the park, he stationed himself on a corner and began to hand them out. It is very difficult to refuse a tract from a man who looks like Ron Rearick, and none of the pamphlets were turned down. By afternoon, Ron had to return to the bookstore for more.

The next day, Sunday, Ron headed to the park once again. This time he not only gave out the tracts—he began to watch how people reacted after they had received them. Some walked away slowly, scanning the words on the leaflets. Some tucked them into pockets or purses. But others, in fact many others, just tossed the tracts aside once they were a few yards away.

Ron began to get really hot. What kind of respect was that, to throw away a message about God's love? Especially when a man had gone and bought that message out of his own paycheck?

Just then a college student accepted a tract, but then crumpled it and tossed it aside just a few yards from Ron. That was a big mistake.

Ron grabbed the kid by the collar. "Hey, fella. Is that all a message from God means to you?" he yelled.

The young man's eyes were wide with shock. Still, he attempted to make a strong stand.

"I don't want to hear about God. I don't believe in Him."

"Oh, really?" Ron asked sarcastically. Still holding the boy's collar, he shook him violently. "Well, it just so happens that there is a God, and He deserves your respect. I want you to pray right now and ask Jesus to come into your life," Ron commanded.

The boy was frowning. Ron lifted the kid off the ground with one hand and gave him a stinging slap with the other. "I said, 'Ask Jesus into your heart!' "

Realizing that this Jesus freak was a real nut, the young man began to obey. Ron the evangelist turned him loose and sent him on his way.[4]

In-your-face Christianity is light that glares. Jesus said, "You are the light of the world. [People don't] light a lamp and put it under a bowl. Instead they put it on its stand, and it gives light to everyone in the house" (Matthew 5:14, 15). That kind of light is useful and welcome. And that's the kind of light Jesus calls us to be—light that glows.

Some years ago in a church where I served as pastor we organized a community event in which people could drive through the Christmas story. The first year of our Living Nativity Drive-Thru we spent three thousand dollars on a mass mailing to twenty thousand homes in the neighborhood. But when we opened for business, nobody came. Finally a few people trickled in. From a questionnaire we discovered that nobody came because of our invitation in the mail. Most of the people who came told us, "I was driving by and saw the commotion," or "So-and-so invited me." Nobody mentioned the mailing.

The next night one of our members rented a four-beam search light. We parked it at the entrance, and from the minute we opened until the minute we closed, we enjoyed bumper to bumper business. That light was a people magnet.

Some people told me, "We didn't even know what this was, but we saw the light, and we got in line." I resisted the urge to tell such people that they needed to get a life. In that four-beam search light we discovered a marketing plan that worked.

It's the same marketing strategy that Jesus calls for in His church. "You are the light in a world of darkness."

LIGHTING THE DARKNESS

Often I am reminded of just how dark the world can be. I think of a conversation I had with the woman next to me on a flight to Amsterdam. After the customary small talk, she told me her story. She was dating a man in Minnesota, so she was returning from spending a couple weeks with him. She said she needed a vacation because she had suffered a great deal of pain in her life over the past few years.

I asked, "What kind of pain? Would you mind sharing with me?"

I could tell this was not going to be easy for her because she started shaking. She said, "I don't like to talk about it without a cigarette to calm me down. It's a long time until we get to Holland, where I can smoke."

I said, "That's fine. You could go to the bathroom and sneak a cigarette and then tell me"—no, I didn't really say that. Rather, she volunteered her story.

"About six months ago, my dad died of lung cancer."

"I'm really sorry to hear that," I said.

"Oh, don't be," she quipped. "To be honest all of us kids were grateful to see him die. For as far back as I can remember he was so abusive to my mom and all seven of us kids. I will always hate the man. Not one of us cried at his funeral.

"Last month my mother committed suicide. She had struggled with depression all her life. She had attempted suicide two times before. Then last August she threw herself into an oncoming train. I cried at her funeral. We were very close.

"Then last month my brother died of cancer."

By this point she was tearing up. I asked her about her religious convictions. "Do you believe in any kind of a hereafter—you know, heaven or purgatory or something?"

"No," she said. "I guess I was kind of raised Catholic, but we never went to church."

So I asked her, "What kind of hope do you have that gets you through all of this heartache? How about a community—you know, a church family or something? How do get through the day?"

She said, "To be honest, I have no hope. I don't belong to a church. I don't believe in a god. I think you live, you die, and that's that."

I don't know how to describe my feelings after that conversation, except to say I felt profoundly sad. It occurred to me during the conversation that the world is so dark. To journey through it with no hope, no community, no future seems so futile.

That's why Jesus called us to a purpose. "You are to be light in a very dark world," He told us. You really can make a difference.

Chuck Colson and Ellen Santilli Vaughn, in their book *The Body*, provide a snapshot of the difference you can make. The setting for this story takes us back to Communist Romania under the dictatorship of Nicolae Ceausescu.

You probably know some of the horror stories that occurred under this sick man's leadership. He starved the people while he feasted on the finest delicacies in his palace in Bucharest. People suffered unspeakable poverty. To build his work force, Ceausescu demanded all Romanian families produce five babies, claiming every fetus as the property of the state.

But Ceausescu's greatest oppression was directed against Christians. He ruled the state church with an iron fist. Most pastors cowered in fear and compromised with the state, but there were some pastors who would not. One such reformed pastor was Laszlo Tokes.

Tokes was a striking man with a thunderous bass voice. He was the interim pastor of an insipid church in the city of Timisoara. The government paid little attention to this Hungarian Reformed Church because it was composed of a handful of old people who were all about to die. But Tokes was about to change all of that.

In his first sermon, Tokes preached that "every person is a light that must shine." His vision ignited a fire among university students. Within two years, the membership of that church swelled to five thousand. Now the government got real nervous. Ceausescu understood that when people take seriously the calling of God to be the light of the world, the result can be blinding. The Romanian secret police knew they could not allow this church to continue. There was no place in Ceausescu's Romania for this flavor of passionate Christian faith.

Meanwhile, Tokes kept preaching: "You are the light of the world," he challenged. "Go shine in the darkness." The government denied Tokes his ration book, preventing him from buying any gas or food. They cut off his phone, except for incoming abusive and threatening calls for which the secret police then charged him long distance fees. They harassed his friends—like the contractor who was putting an extension on the church balcony. His dead body was found in Timisoara Park. They stabbed Tokes in the face.

But Tokes kept preaching to his congregation, "You are the light of the world. Go and let your light shine in a dark place." And his church members were doing it. They didn't seem to care if they were tortured or killed; they let their light shine.

The secret police did not want to kill Tokes for fear of making him a martyr, so they opted instead to exile him to a small, remote village outside of Timisoara. The exile was scheduled for December 15, 1989.

On December 10, Tokes announced, "I have been issued a summons of eviction. I will not accept it, so I will be taken from you by force next Friday."

The following Friday, the secret police came to Tokes's apartment in the church, but they could not get near it because thousands of church members stood as a human shield around that church.

The people chanted, "We are one in Christ. We are one. We are one in Christ."

The mayor of Timisoara addressed the crowd, promising that Tokes could stay if they would go home. The crowd responded by saying, "We don't believe you." They would not budge.

At 1:00 A.M., Tokes glanced out his window, and he could not believe his eyes. Light from thousands of candles pierced the darkness. The candles burned through the night and into the following day. On through the next night the street was still ablaze with thousands of flickering flames.

Finally the police stormed into the church and captured Tokes's wife. They stabbed her, then whisked her away. They could not find Tokes because he was hiding under the Communion table. The police opened fire on the crowd, murdering hundreds of Christians.

By Christmas that year, the world applauded the courage of Christians who took that stand. Romania was free, and Ceausescu was gone.

A few days after Christmas, a boy named Daniel Gavra was recuperating after being shot in the protest. He resembled a mummy with his bandaged wounds. He had a stump where his left leg had been. But his spirit was strong. His pastor, Peter Dugulescu, came to visit him. Daniel said to his pastor, "I don't mind so much the loss of my leg. After all, it was I who lit the first candle." Daniel Gavra reminds us that it is possible to change the destiny of nations through the light of one candle.[5]

God has put you in a very dark world that is starving for His grace. That's why you are here. You can make a difference. Go light the world.

Go Out Like a Light
(Questions for Reflection or Group Study)

1. If you were to describe yourself in terms of light, what kind of light would you be? Why?
2. When do you feel most purposeful in life? Can you relate to Warren Schmidt's experience of finding meaning in helping others?

3. What is the connection between a person's character and his or her influence?
4. Make a list of other metaphors (other than salt or light) that might describe kingdom people.
5. Share of a time when you received news that was so good you couldn't keep it to yourself. Do you suppose that if we fully understood the gospel, our compulsion to share would be similar? Why or why not?
6. Give examples of light that glares and light that glows.
7. How can your church be a lighthouse?
8. Make a covenant in your group to light up our dark world this week. Discuss specific things that you can do to be "the light of the world."
9. How do you want to be remembered? What do you hope people say about you at your funeral?

1. Malcolm Muggeridge in "Jesus Rediscovered," *Christianity Today,* vol. 41, no. 11.

2. William Barclay, *The Gospel of Matthew,* vol. 1 (Philadelphia: The Westminster Press, 1975) p. 123.

3. Sheldon Vanauken, *A Severe Mercy* (New York: Harper & Row, 1977), p. 85, quoted on <http://www.swd.lcms.org/schools/prnews/prnews02-04.htm>.

4. Ron Rearick and Mari Hanes, *Iceman: The Story of Ron Rearick* (Helena, Mont.: Falcon Press Publishing Company, 1982), p. 73.

5. Charles Colson and Ellen Santilli Vaughn, *The Body* (Dallas, Tex.: Word Publishing, 1992), pp. 51–61.

Conclusion

On a recent trip to New York City, I ventured off Broadway and caught the play *Tuesdays with Morrie*. Having read the book, I was curious about Liberty Theatre's adaptation for the stage.

The book camped on the *New York Times* bestseller list for years. It's the story of an ambitious sports reporter, Mitch Albom, who is reunited with his former mentor and college professor, Morrie Schwartz. After seeing Ted Koppel interview Morrie on *Nightline,* Mitch discovers that his former professor is dying from Lou Gehrig's disease. So every Tuesday Mitch would fly from Detroit to Boston to learn from this old man. Their rekindled relationship turned into one final "class"—lessons in how to live.

The play proved as entertaining as the book. There was only one glitch—for the first fifteen minutes, a high-pitched squeal pierced our ears. Turning to my friend, Jim, I whispered, "What is that noise? It's driving me crazy!"

"Me too," Jim answered. "Maybe it's the P.A. system or a hearing aid or something."

Suddenly a fracas erupted below us. From the front row of the balcony, Jim and I had a bird's eye view of the action. An animated usher was earnestly tugging on the arm of an elderly woman.

Meanwhile, on stage, the actor portraying Mitch Albom tried to continue his monologue. But then he snapped. Breaking character, he barked in the direction of the commotion, "Excuse me, but are you about finished over there?" Gaining confidence from the crowd, the actor then berated the lady and insisted that she be dismissed.

At first I thought perhaps it was part of the play, but I soon realized this was no act. The house lights came on as the usher demanded, "Lady, you must come with me."

"Get your #^*%#*! hands off of me," she screamed.

"You must leave this theater right now. Your hearing aid is preventing others from enjoying the performance."

The audience applauded wildly. One man jeered in a thick Brooklyn accent, "Beat it lady, before we all throw you out of here."

"OK, OK," the woman sighed as she struggled to escape the cushioned seat. "I'll leave, but don't you touch me." As she slowly shuffled toward the exit, most everyone cheered.

The play resumed. It was a stirring story of how much this dying old man, Morrie, had to offer—even after he became totally dependant on the care of others. He lost all of his biological functions, and yet Mitch discovered there was still so much in him to be valued.

The final curtain call sparked a prolonged, standing ovation. Mitch and Morrie smiled, bowed, hugged each other, and blew kisses at adoring fans.

But I couldn't applaud. Oh, the acting was fine. The dialogue was crisp. The staging was clean. The plot crescendoed to a fitting climax. Still, I couldn't clap.

My heart was still bleeding for the hearing-impaired woman. *How ironic*, I thought, *that we have just spent ninety minutes being reminded of how much elderly people matter, and yet when we had a perfect opportunity to put the play into practice by treating that older lady with respect, we slam-dunked her instead. We listened to her needs with deaf ears.*

I still wonder, *What value is there in watching an act if there's no redemptive action that follows?* To press my concern into the context of this book, I wonder: *What value is there in reading a book on soul matters if it makes no matter to your soul?* The value of your journey through these pages depends on how you live today . . . and tomorrow. Will your time commitments today reflect what you value most? Can your soul find rest, trusting fully in God, even when pain prevails? Are you intentional about nurturing your soul through community? And will you enrich your soul by spilling out your life in loving service to others?

"He that hath ears to hear, let him hear" (Matthew 11:15, KJV).

You'll want to read these other books by Karl Haffner!

The Cure for Soul Fatigue
Weariness of soul is epidemic. The unmerciful crush of life's demands drains the hope and meaning out of life and keeps us from reaching our full potential. With lots of laugh therapy along the way and mega-doses of wisdom, pastor and author Karl Haffner exposes the root causes of soul fatigue and prescribes the biblical cures to remedy them.
0-8163-1840-9. Paper. 128 pages.
US$10.99, Can$16.49.

Pilgrim's Problems
We are all spiritual pilgrims on a journey to God's front door. And if we're honest, progress on that journey can be slow. Stuff gets in the way and trips us up. Stuff like greed, failure, loneliness, anger, guilt, and pride. Pastor Haffner has good news: "The battle is not in trying to stop sinning. The battle is in trying to keep trusting. God does the changing. We do the trusting."
0-8163-2022-5. Paper. 144 pages.
US$11.99, Can$17.99.

The Cure for the Last Daze
This book is written for seekers not scholars. It's for those who desire a working understanding of the events leading up to the apocalypse. It's for the apocalyptically challenged who are serious about being ready when Jesus comes.
0-8163-1960-X. Paper, 144 pages.
US$6.97, Can.$9.47.